The Athlete Apperception Technique

As the field of sport psychology has matured, so a greater appreciation for a diversity of training models, research methodologies, and therapeutic approaches, opposed to the dominant models of objective testing, has developed. *The Athlete Apperception Technique* (AAT) sets out a sport-specific projective test for practitioners working in sport and exercise service delivery or counselling work with athletes and coaches.

This innovative book includes

- a basic primer on projective methods and the psychoanalytic theory behind them;
- a history of projective, storytelling instruments in clinical psychology;
- the development of the image set for the AAT;
- some examples of interpreting AAT image stories;
- instructions for the administration of the AAT;
- a scoring guide for the stories produced;
- and in-depth descriptions of the stimulus properties of each image in the AAT, along with all images presented as full-page illustrations.

The AAT will help sport practitioners identify and assess personality features, relationships, anxieties, achievement, motivation, and perfectionism, and augment the recent shift in orientation for service delivery to athletes and provide a more in-depth understanding of athletes' characters. The AAT is useful supplementary reading for students of sport psychology and a novel tool for any practicing sport psychologist.

Petah M. Gibbs is based in Melbourne, Australia, and works as a psychology and high performance consultant for several professional sporting clubs and leagues in Australia and the USA (including AFL, NBL, WNBL, NBA, NCAA). His main areas of interest are in coach and player welfare, professional and personal development, career transition, and character profiling (recruiting).

Mark B. Andersen is a professor in the School of Health and Welfare at Halmstad University in Sweden and a clinical psychologist in private practice in Hobart, Tasmania, Australia. His interests include the application of psychodynamic theory in sport and clinical practice, mindfulness and Buddhist psychology, neuropsychotherapy, sport injuries, and quantitative and qualitative research methods.

Daryl B. Marchant is a registered psychologist and associate professor in the College of Sport and Exercise Science and the Institute of Sport, Exercise, and Active Living at Victoria University in Melbourne, Australia. His research, publications, and supervision interests include applied sport psychology, psychometrics, personality, choking in sport, psychological profiling, and coach development.

Routledge Research in Sport and Exercise Science

The *Routledge Research in Sport and Exercise Science* series is a showcase for cutting-edge research from across the sport and exercise sciences, including physiology, psychology, biomechanics, motor control, physical activity and health, and every core sub-discipline. Featuring the work of established and emerging scientists and practitioners from around the world, and covering the theoretical, investigative and applied dimensions of sport and exercise, this series is an important channel for new and ground-breaking research in the human movement sciences.

Available in this series

Life Story Research in Sport
Understanding the Experiences of Elite and Professional Athletes through Narrative
Kitrina Douglas and David Carless

The Psychology of Doping in Sport
Edited by Vassilis Barkoukis, Lambros Lazuras and Haralambos Tsorbatzoudis

Complex Systems in Sport
Edited by Keith Davids, Robert Hristovski, Duarte Araújo, Natalia Balague Serre, Chris Button and Pedro Passos

Detecting Doping in Sport
Stephen Moston and Terry Engelberg

The Science of Climbing and Mountaineering
Edited by Ludovic Seifert, Peter Wolf and Andreas Schweizer

The Athlete Apperception Technique
Manual and Materials for Sport and Clinical Psychologists
Petah M. Gibbs, Mark B. Andersen and Daryl B. Marchant

The Athlete Apperception Technique

Manual and Materials for Sport and Clinical Psychologists

Petah M. Gibbs, Mark B. Andersen and Daryl B. Marchant

LONDON AND NEW YORK

First published 2017 by Routledge

2 Park Square, Milton Park, Abingdon, Oxon OX14 4RN
605 Third Avenue, New York, NY 10017

Routledge is an imprint of the Taylor & Francis Group, an informa business

First issued in paperback 2021

Publisher's Note

The publisher has gone to great lengths to ensure the quality of this reprint but points out that some imperfections in the original copies may be apparent.

British Library Cataloguing-in-Publication Data
A catalogue record for this book is available from the British Library

Library of Congress Cataloguing-in-Publication Data
A catalog record for this book has been requested

ISBN: 978-1-138-24413-9 (hbk)
ISBN: 978-0-367-40783-4 (pbk)

Typeset in Times New Roman
by Apex CoVantage, LLC

This manual is dedicated to my family and friends who do their best to tolerate me.

Petah Mingo Gibbs

For all the sport and exercise psychology crew in my Scandinavian home at Halmstad Högskolan in Sweden.

Mark Bille Andersen

To Tina, I love you just the way you are, have been and will become.

Daryl B. Marchant

Contents

Figures

Tables

Acknowledgement

Thanks to Kerri Gibbs who created and refined the AAT images. Please check out her other excellent work at www.portraitartist.com/gibbs/.

Introduction

To "peel back the onion" is a commonly used metaphor in psychology. Just as the process of peeling the onion back layer-by-layer gradually reveals the core and flavour of the onion, the psychologist seeks to understand the psychological core of a client, including personality, motives, and life issues. Each layer of the onion can also metaphorically represent the constructions that protect a person's core. One of the most fascinating aspects of psychological practice is the tremendous range of theories, techniques, and interventions that are legitimately and expertly used as therapy to *peel back* and examine the complexities of each client.

This manual presents the theoretical foundations for projective testing and assessment and introduces and outlines the development of a sport-specific projective instrument, the *Athlete Apperception Technique* (AAT). We developed the AAT to be used in sport and exercise psychology service delivery and research along with applications in clinical and applied psychology with athletes and coaches. As with the onion, the AAT is layered. We will take the reader, chapter by chapter, through the layers and reveal a technique that, although relatively new in sport psychology, is founded on layers of research, practice, and evidence in mainstream psychology accumulated over decades. We hope to engage readers in a process that will exercise the mind and muscles that perhaps first stimulated them to engage in the field of sport psychology.

We hope to challenge your thinking, as you, in turn, will undoubtedly challenge elements of our AAT. We ask you to activate the skills and attributes that effective psychologists possess, including curiosity, reflection, lateral thinking, intuition, patience, open-mindedness, and inductive reasoning.

This introduction is structured to achieve four purposes: first, to briefly describe the essentials of the AAT; second, to discuss the reasons why the AAT can benefit sport and exercise psychologists irrespective of their theoretical orientations; third, to outline key points of consideration when using the AAT; and fourth, to provide the rationale for each subsequent chapter.

We are confident time invested in better comprehending the AAT will be rewarded with a rich understanding of an approach that, for various reasons, has remained at the near-invisible fringes of sport and exercise psychology literature and practice.

We also appreciate that therapy itself, once stripped of its layers, is essentially about assisting clients to develop insight, cope with life, function more effectively, and achieve their goals. For the AAT to be useful to practitioners, these links and connections to the primary purposes of psychotherapy (and most interpersonal psychological treatments including psychological skills training) must be apparent. To this end, we provide case examples and associated narratives of how the AAT has been used with clients. For those interested in projective test construction, we provide details of the many steps taken to develop and refine the AAT. This manual will provide the interested sport and exercise psychologist with the necessary tools to use the AAT appropriately, ethically, and competently.

What is the Athlete Apperception Technique?

The significance of this manual is the development and dissemination of a projective assessment tool specifically for use within sport and exercise settings. The AAT was conceptualised as a derivative of the Thematic Apperception Technique (TAT). The TAT was developed by Henry Murray and Christina Morgan in 1934 and remains to this day a popular assessment tool in psychology. Similar to the TAT, the AAT is inspired from psychodynamic foundations and fits within the projective testing genre. Both the TAT and the AAT comprise images (referred to as *cards* in the TAT) depicting ambiguous situations. The images used in the TAT are a collection of photographs, paintings, and drawings; in the AAT we have used original sketches based on a variety of sporting situations (see Chapter 2). The AAT was produced using the TAT as a blueprint and is a derivative of the original, but with sports people as the population in mind. The final primary set of AAT images consists of 10 images. Two further sets of images are also provided: a supplementary set of 5 images (AAT-S) and a children's set of 6 images (AAT-C). In Chapter 3, we explain the stimulus properties of the images and identify themes that are commonly "pulled" from each image by sport psychologists intending to pursue particular themes with clients. Depending on the administrative purpose, clients or participants are asked to construct a story for each image. These images and the explanatory stories clients construct, facilitate the use of projection, a psychodynamic process identified by Freud that taps unconscious thoughts, feelings, and motivations. Freud (1895/1962) explained that projection is a process of ascribing one's drives, feelings, and sentiments to other people or the outside world as a defensive tactic that allows one to remain unaware of these undesirable phenomena in oneself. Projection is perhaps best situated or recognised as an ego defence mechanism.

Developed by Morgan and Murray at the Harvard Psychological Institute in the early 1930s, the TAT is typically used to investigate the dynamics of personality. Morgan and Murray were influenced by a psychodynamic approach to personality (Teglasi, 2001), and they regarded their interpretations of the TAT stories as a psychodynamic process. Using projective techniques, such as the TAT in therapeutic settings, enables the clinician to gain insights into how the dynamics of personality are manifested in interpersonal relations and how clients describe and interpret their environments. Regarding the TAT, Murray (1938) concluded, "the test is based on the well-recognized fact that when a person interprets an ambiguous social situation, he is apt to expose his personality as much as the phenomenon to which he is attending" (p. 530). Respondents provide explanatory stories that include common themes such as the relationships among the characters, feelings and actions of the characters, evaluations of the characters, preceding events, and possible outcomes. Psychodynamically oriented clinicians use projective assessments to gain insights into a client's dynamics of personality, motivations, and interpersonal dynamics. Murray (1938) stated, "If the procedure had merely exposed conscious fantasies and remembered events it would have been useful enough, but it did more than this. It gave the experimenter excellent clues for the divination of unconscious thematic formations" (p. 534). Murray believed clients are largely unaware they are talking about themselves and that their conscious defences were bypassed. We believe the AAT provides a unique therapeutic tool for sport psychologists to expose athletes' unconscious foundations of their personalities, fantasies, and resistances.

How can the AAT benefit sport and exercise psychologists?

The AAT was developed with the applied sport and exercise psychologist in mind. We (the authors) have all spent considerable time in providing applied sport psychology services to recreational, sub-elite, and elite/professional athletes across a wide spectrum of sports. Based on our experiences, we are confident that the AAT provides a means to holistically understand athletes, their personalities, motivations, performance themes, challenges, and life histories. Our objective from the outset has been to develop the AAT to the point that it can be used in research and applied settings. We also intend that the AAT can best contribute to sport psychological knowledge when findings are integrated with multiple sources of data (e.g., questionnaires, intake interviews). The AAT should specifically help sport practitioners identify and assess personality features, sources of stress, interpersonal relations, motivations, attributional styles, fears, hopes, and perfectionistic tendencies.

The AAT will appeal to sport psychologists and their clients who desire to dig deeper and are not necessarily enslaved to the dominant sport psychology cognitive-behavioural paradigm. The growth of sport psychology has largely coincided with an era dominated by "objective" (i.e., quantitative) testing and alternative assessment options are limited (e.g., behavioural observations, intake interviews). With the increasing maturation of the field of sport and exercise psychology, there appears to be a greater appreciation for the diversity of training models, research methodologies, and therapeutic approaches other than the cognitive-behavioural model. For example, psychodynamic formulations and interpretations have begun to appear more frequently in the sport psychology literature. We believe the timing is right to introduce a sport-specific projective technique that facilitates in-depth case conceptualisations of athlete and coaches that go beyond the dominant, but sometimes limited, cognitive-behavioural sport psychology service paradigm.

We believe applied sport psychologists are likely to find the AAT relatively adaptable to different purposes and situations. First, the AAT can be profitably used as a supplement to standard intake interviews where the practitioner is working toward a broad understanding of their clients and their presenting issues. Because the AAT images are normally presented to clients as ambiguous scenarios with no right or wrong answers, they provide a stimulus for clients to provide a narrative of sporting themes they are readily familiar with. When using the AAT as a supplement to standard question-and-answer intake techniques, we recommend that a few selected cards be chosen, or the that the client be given a choice over which card or cards they prefer to interpret. We expect practitioners will feel that the inclusion of AAT cards provides an interesting additional source of information from which to form working hypotheses and case formulations. Similarly, case conceptualisation can be enhanced with the abundant convergent and sometimes divergent information derived from AAT stories clients provide.

Second, the AAT is especially well suited to working with clients who either have limited insight, who are resistant, who struggle to clearly identify their primary issues, or who experience re-occurring negative patterns of behaviour. Because the AAT taps unconscious motivations and attributes of personality, the process of projection, albeit often unrecognised by the client, provides the experienced practitioner with plenty of therapeutic "grist for the mill." For instances when a traumatic sporting event or outcome has been repressed, themes such as abuse or discrimination in their various forms are sometimes difficult for clients to discuss openly. The AAT potentially provides an alternative and less threatening means by which difficult themes might be discussed, identified, and later explored.

Third, because the large majority of AAT images involves two or more characters, the resultant stories provide ample material from which to draw inferences about how the client portrays other people and interpersonal relations. For example, in some images, stories that include references to important or significant others, such as parents, team-mates, or coaches can provide sub-theme contents such as nurturance, support, authority, or communication. Because interpersonal relationships are important for athlete functioning and performance, AAT images can provide useful clues about how athletes respond in varying interpersonal circumstances such as both harmonious and strained relationships.

Fourth, the AAT provides diversity and originality in a field where arguably original and creative assessment techniques seem limited. There is a large body of research and development in psychology dedicated to psychological assessments. The majority of those assessment instruments are pencil and paper tests with the minority of them designed as visual or pictorial. Of course, psychological tests and assessments are central to the work of many psychologists across educational, clinical, forensic, counselling, organisational, and sport domains. Nowadays, psychological testing and assessment are often associated with commercial aspects of psychological practice, are tightly controlled and protected, and are sometimes contentious. Test developers are expected to create measures that are theoretically driven, psychometrically sound, and evidence based. Furthermore, effective psychological measures need to be administered and scored in a time-efficient manner and are robust against biases, such as impression management and social desirability. We have constructed the AAT as a technique rather than a test per se and do not plan to develop it as a highly commercialised product. As previously stated, our main objective is to provide an alternative means of working with athletes to what has traditionally been used and accepted. Nevertheless, the AAT is not, nor should it be, immune to the expectations that the technique is sound from theoretical, best practice, or assessment perspectives. The following chapters will demonstrate that the AAT is based on a strong foundation of psychoanalytic theory dating back to Freud and the early pioneers of psychodynamic psychology (e.g., Rorschach).

Fifth, the AAT and the telling and re-telling of the stories between the psychologist and the athlete can act, in itself, as a means for therapeutic understanding and change as the insights gleaned from the AAT may help athletes re-story their lives in more salubrious and happier ways than they did before. We expect that the process of deconstructing, reconstructing, discussing, and understanding stories provides a self-rewarding means of developing personal and professional insights for both client and therapist.

Considerations for sport and clinical psychologists intending to use the AAT

For sport and clinical psychologists employing the AAT, there are numerous abilities and skills that need to be harnessed. For example, the following attributes and skills are undoubtedly helpful: building and maintaining rapport, deductive and inductive thinking, looking beyond the facts, empathy, understanding motivators for behaviour, personal insight, self-reflection, and active listening. Many of these skills and abilities are not dissimilar to what a detective might possess. Patience, for instance, is important both in understanding how to administer and assess the AAT data and especially in building case histories that highlight prominent response themes. Nevertheless, as with most psychological tests, techniques, and interventions, effort spent developing personal expertise will yield rich rewards over time with repeated use. Personal insight is an important barometer in identifying aspects of stories that particularly resonate, coalesce, frighten, or conflict with the psychologist's personal history. Time spent in self-reflection during or between AAT administrations can provide the opportunities for the therapist's unconscious mind to make useful associations, connections, and, of course, projections.

In working with clients, we are particularly drawn to the concept of client and therapist journeying together much like traveller and guide. The experienced guide will assess the goals and fitness of the traveller (akin to therapeutic intake and assessment) at the outset. For example, Petitpas (2000) took the phrase *pace before you lead* from Lankton (1980), in discussing the importance of "matching or attending to the athlete's present focus before attempting to lead him or her in a new direction" (p. 36). For us, we think of *pacing* as walking beside the athlete; getting to know the whole story of how the athlete functions in and out of sport; finding out the athletes' histories and the contingencies of reinforcement and punishment they experience in their different psychosocial environments. We believe the AAT is especially helpful as a tool in the early stages of the therapeutic journey to explore athlete hopes, dreams, anxieties, and barriers to happiness. We also aim to become a friendly ally and travelling companion as we navigate their intra- and interpersonal landscapes together and travel forward by guiding, helping and *leading* them to happier and healthier places. We have often seen sport and clinical psychologists with problem-focused approaches where an athlete presents a concern (e.g., competitive anxiety) and quite soon after that presentation outcomes an intervention (e.g., relaxation, cognitive restructuring) that seems premature because the symptom of something like competitive anxiety is almost always part of a much bigger picture than sport or competition. The AAT can provide invaluable meta-indicators of how clients interpret their present. These indicators often include information and projections that are normally difficult to access and can greatly inform how practitioners choose to *lead*.

Constructing the AAT (and the production of this manual) has been a labour of love for us, and our biases towards a psychodynamic understanding of sport persons are manifest, but one does not have to be dynamically oriented to use the AAT. In our view, irrespective of the theoretical orientation or practicing paradigm that practitioners subscribe to, the AAT can potentially unearth valuable information. We also believe that practitioners adopting the AAT will find the rewards to be commensurate with the time invested in learning and using the AAT (see Chapter 7). Our main hope, however, is that practitioners will find the AAT helpful in their endeavours to connect with their clients and help them along their paths.

References

Freud, S. (1962). On the grounds for detaching a particular syndrome from neurasthenia under the description "anxiety neurosis." In J. Strachey (Trans. & Ed.), *The standard edition of the complete psychological works of Sigmund Freud* (Vol. III, pp. 87–115). London, England: Hogarth Press. (Original work published 1895.)

Lankton, S. R. (1980). *Practical magic: A translation of basic neurolinguistic programming into clinical psychotherapy*. Cupertino, CA: Meta.

Murray, H. A. (1938). *Explorations in personality: A clinical and experimental study of fifty men of college age*. New York, NY: Oxford University Press.

Petitpas, A. J. (2000). *Managing stress on and off the field: The littlefoot approach to learned resourcefulness*. In M. B. Andersen (Ed.), *Doing sport psychology* (pp. 33–43). Champaign, IL: Human Kinetics.

Teglasi, H. (2001). *Essentials of the TAT and other storytelling techniques assessment*. New York, NY: Wiley.

1 Projective techniques[1]

The development of early projective techniques was strongly influenced by the psychoanalytic movement. According to Rabin (1986), clinical psychologists, pre-1930, had few assessment tools (e.g., the Stanford-Binet, some personality inventories of limited range). Essentially the clinicians of this era mainly used quantitative indices, IQs, percentiles on introversion or dominance scales, and similar pieces of nomothetic information. Rabin suggested the introduction of projective techniques gave clinicians the opportunity to communicate something meaningful to professional colleagues about the personality structure, dynamics, and diagnoses of clients. Results from projective techniques also contributed to the planning of therapeutic processes. According to Rabin, the clinical tradition provided a setting for the development of projective techniques, and today projective tests remain favoured instruments of many clinical psychologists and common methods of assessing personality.

As early as 1907, a simple projective technique consisting of a series of pictures was available for personality assessment of children. Since the early 1900s, the use of psychodynamically driven personality tests has waxed and waned. For example, in the 1920s and 1930s, there were ground-breaking developments such as the Rorschach Inkblot Test (Rorschach, 1921) and the Thematic Apperception Test (TAT, Morgan & Murray, 1935). These classic early personality tests are still widely used and have spawned a huge number of derivative techniques. A gradual shift took place when the development and popularity of self-report tests led to a reappraisal, and in some instances scepticism, of older projective methods. During the 1950s, many psychologists were strident in asserting that projective techniques did not meet established psychometric criteria of reliability and validity.

The popularity of sport psychology as a specific discipline has largely coincided with an era dominated by quantitative (often self-report) testing (1960s to present). Like mainstream psychologists, some sport psychologists use various tests and techniques to assess personality. The many instruments that have been developed to assess personality in sport are predominantly quantitative/self-report measures. With the increasing maturation of the field of sport psychology, there appears to be a growing appreciation for diversity of training models, research methodologies, and other approaches beyond the dominant cognitive-behavioural paradigm. For example, psychodynamic interpretations and formulations have begun to appear relatively frequently in the sport psychology literature (Andersen, 2005; Andersen, Barney, & Waterson, 2016; Strean & Strean, 1998).

Historical traces and theoretical foundations

Freud introduced the term *projection* (e.g., Freud, 1896/1953). He stated that projection is a process of ascribing one's own drives, feelings, and sentiments to other people or the outside world as a defensive tactic that allows one to remain unaware of these undesirable phenomena in oneself. Murray (1938) first introduced the term *projection test* in a ground-breaking study titled *Explorations in Personality*. The term is the generic label for a collection of varied psychological assessment tools. This collection includes inkblot methods (e.g., Rorschach), storytelling methods (e.g., TAT), drawing techniques (e.g., human figure drawing, house-tree-person), and verbal stimuli techniques (e.g., sentence completion, word association). Murray described these methods as, "an attempt to discover the covert (inhibited) and unconscious (partially repressed) tendencies of normal persons . . . simply different methods of stimulating imaginative processes and facilitating their expression in words or in action" (p. 248).

As discussed briefly in the Introduction, one of the most accepted and widely used projective techniques to investigate the dynamics of personality is the TAT (Morgan & Murray, 1935), which involves a psychodynamic process of interpretation. Using the TAT in a therapeutic setting enables clinicians to gain insights into how the dynamics of personality are manifested in interpersonal relations, and how clients describe and interpret their environments. The TAT consists of 30 cards (and one blank card) with the majority of images depicting people in a variety of life situations. Clients are asked to interpret the scene by identifying the central (main) character, telling what is taking place, describing the thoughts and feelings of the characters, recounting events leading to the scene, and telling what the outcome will be. Clients reveal their personal apperception of the images through the medium of *projection*. They project onto the images their own hopes, dreams, fears, frustrations, relationship, and so forth.

Interpreting projective techniques

Clinicians working with the TAT differ in how they use the tool as source material for finding characteristics of their clients they believe are significant. For example, a clinician may use the TAT solely to determine diagnostic characterisations of behaviour, or to locate important emotional relationships in a person's world. According to Rotter (1946), interpretations from the TAT should be considered only as hypotheses or leads for further investigation, and "the value, significance, nature, and validity of the tests are dependent upon the interpreter, his experience, and his approach to the field of personality" (p. 206).

Interpretation can include identifying the "degree" of projection (how much projection is going on) and complementing responses with case notes of interactions with clients. Adcock (1965) suggested that practitioners should appreciate the difficulty of interpreting the degree of projection involved in a client's storytelling. Adcock warned against practitioners relying on the mere counting of needs and conflicts and being too concerned with group averages. The interaction between the clinician and client is a central component of the interpretation process and understanding the degree of projection.

The problem with most projective tests is almost always the same; they allow the interpreter to project as much as the client. The interpretation of respondents' stories requires clinicians to be highly aware of their needs and projections. According to Killian and Campbell (1992), transference and counter-transference also play important roles in the interpretation of clients' stories. Eron (1959) suggested there is a tendency to distort in storytelling due to the effects of transference. For example, clients may make conscious (or unconscious) efforts to please practitioners and present themselves as specific kinds of persons. There may also be a tendency for practitioners to misinterpret the meaning of stories due to a lack of awareness, or analysis, of their own counter-transference. For example, if clients have some behaviours or personality features that remind practitioners (unconsciously) of others in the past who have disappointed them, then there may be a tendency to interpret the stories in a more negative light than if clients remind professionals of positive past experiences with significant others. We discuss the issues of practitioner projection, transference, and counter-transference as "special considerations and limitations during administration" in more detail in Chapter 4.

Validity and reliability

Projective techniques have been a matter of concern to psychometricians because they do not conform to the usual methods of establishing reliability and validity. Critics have pointed to validity problems (or limitations) of projective techniques especially when interpretation is not based on quantified scores or normative data, and have dismissed their usefulness as personality assessment techniques. According to Jensen (1959), "if the TAT is short on actual validity, it certainly is not lacking in what might be called *subjective validity* (akin to *faith validity*)" (p. 312). Jensen suggested some psychologists have greater capacities than others for experiencing subjective validity. This capacity seems to be associated with training and experience in psychoanalysis, psychotherapy, and projective techniques in general. Jensen also asserted that one reason for the survival of the TAT in clinical practice is this subjective validity. "While research has shown the TAT to have low reliability and negligible validity, many clinical psychologists continue to use it, apparently with some satisfaction" (Jensen, 1959, p. 313). Applying the rules of quantitative test validation to projective techniques, however, is a misapplication. Trying to fit the TAT into a quantitative psychometric mode is akin to applying quantitative positivist paradigms to qualitative research such as ethnography and life histories. It is an unfair comparison, and it misses the point that projective techniques are clinical instruments designed to help us understand people.

Projective assessment in sport

There is a prevailing trend in sport psychology to focus on observable and self-reported traits of athletes. According to Apitzsch (1995), trait theory and social learning theory have received the most attention in sport personality research, whereas, little attention has been given to psychodynamic theory. An advocate of psychodynamic therapy for athletes, Cratty (1989) suggested that the interpretation of athletes' dreams is useful in conjunction with projective tools to "assess such concepts as achievement needs in sports, aggressive reactions to frustrating sports situations, and perhaps anxiety in sporting contexts. Projective tools have existed for decades, but they were not designed with the specifics of sport in mind" (p. 37). The interpretation of projective techniques, according to Cratty, may differ depending on the tester and test environment. Individuals may also fluctuate in their responses to visual stimuli depending on external factors during administration. These differences and fluctuations, however, are useful because they may provide a great deal of information for the clinician. As Cratty stated, "Projective tests give breadth and depth to clinical psychology. Fortunately, they are not dead" (p. 36). Although Cratty appears pleased that projective tests have not died, these techniques have been in a serious slumber.

There have been few serious attempts over the last 20 years to develop a projective technique for use in a sport context (see Chapter 2 for more history on projective techniques developed for sport), but there have been studies of athletes using projective methods. Although there are some prevailing opinions on the usefulness of a sport-specific projective technique, a few sport psychology researchers have found projective techniques to be, at least, useful means of gathering information. For example, Benzi and Michelini (1987) administered a series of projective techniques with the aim of describing the psychological profiles of artistic roller skaters. Johnson, Hutton, and Johnson (1954) also attempted to describe and measure the personality traits of "champion" athletes using projective techniques. Although these two examples demonstrate some applications of projective techniques in sport, further examples of researchers using projective techniques in sport settings are extremely rare. Often the criticism of using projective techniques focuses on the belief that information is based on dated research and literature. In particular, the criticism that arises from sport researchers and clinicians is often sourced from information found outside of the sport literature. Projective techniques are readily available as sources of complementary information but not as an all-encompassing answer to personality dynamics. Clinicians may expect too much from this one source rather than taking a projective technique as part of a battery of personality assessment tools (a holistic view of assessment).

There remain differing opinions regarding the use of projective techniques in sport psychology service delivery (e.g., Cox, 2007; Cratty, 1989). These differences appear to hinge on two primary points: (a) the value of the instruments as tools in collecting information about athletes that is not easily obtained with self-report techniques, and (b) the psychometric adequacy of the instruments. In specific reference to point (b), opponents focus on psychometric inadequacies of projective techniques, and proponents focus on the potential usefulness of such instruments. Proponents also point out that projective techniques allow considerable freedom for clients to generate responses that provide information about their psychological constitutions.

Projective techniques are attractive as clinical tools, but they are often difficult to score and interpret. Projective techniques were, however, not originally designed or intended for quantitative studies. Cratty (1989) suggested that they provide insightful information for psychologists and researchers, but are not suited for statistical inferences for athletic populations; rather, "they are tools for clinical psychologists and psychiatrists who are both intuitive and expert" (p. 36). Essentially, the use of projective techniques gives practitioners a means to gain insight into a patient's innermost feelings and current conflicts and needs. Cox (2007) maintained a more traditional psychometric approach to sport psychology assessment. According to Cox, projective techniques are "unstructured," allowing people to be open and honest in their responses. He suggested that projective methods are not often used by sport psychologists, but that is not to say they should not be used.

In reference to the TAT, in particular, Cox suggested, "its validity and reliability are highly dependent upon the skill and training of the individual administering and interpreting the results" (p. 26). In the field of projective testing, problems of validation are particularly salient. Anzieu (1960) maintained that projective tests, "do not explore a single variable, but describe an individual in terms of a dynamic system where the variables themselves are in inter-correlation" (p. 217). Projective techniques do, however, provide an alternative to nomothetic approaches to assessment. (For further discussion, see Chapter 5.)

Although there has been widespread resistance to projective techniques in sport psychology (and to some extent the psychological community as a whole) since the 1950s, the premise that projective technique use has limited application is questionable. According to Lazarus (1989), all assessment and treatment of human problems should be holistic, or totalistic, as exemplified by multimodal therapy. Multimodal therapy involves an assessment of the individual using the integration of different but interrelated modalities or psychological parameters (e.g., behaviour, physiology, cognition, interpersonal relationships, sensation, imagery, affect). In other words, the use of multiple assessment tools and divergent theoretical approaches when assessing an individual can only enhance the understanding of the individual's needs, motives, and drives.

In describing personality, psychologists have relied heavily on developing, administering, and interpreting personality tests and techniques. It is difficult to measure personality directly, but projective techniques provide an opportunity for people to describe their feelings and thoughts about a range of stimuli. For example, someone might be shown a photo of an exhausted runner crossing a finishing line at the end of a track race and be asked to write about what is happening. A high-achieving, confident person might emphasise how the runner made an effort to achieve a goal, whereas a low-achiever might project feelings of disappointment at losing the race in a close finish. An athlete can answer any pencil and paper tests, or interview questions (self-report methods) with verbal and conscious decisions. There may be, however, unconscious motives that cannot be measured on self-report inventories. A well-trained and intuitive clinician may pick up the conflict through discussion, but projective methods can be effective techniques to assist the athlete in (unconsciously) sharing such information.

This brief chapter serves as a kind of launching pad for an account of how we went about developing the Athlete Apperception Technique. The controversies and debates around projective testing will probably continue as long as there are projective instruments, and we hope that the AAT will stimulate debate within sport and exercise psychology concerning the some of the ways we go about trying to understand the people we serve and help them along their paths. For those currently doubtful about projective techniques, we simply request that they exercise the type of open-minded approach that can engender all types of possibilities (and also experiment with the technique firsthand).

Note

1 Most of this chapter was previously published as: Gibbs, P. M. (2010). Psychological assessment: Projective techniques. In S. J. Hanrahan & M. B. Andersen (Eds.), *Routledge handbook of applied sport psychology: A comprehensive guide for students and practitioners* (pp. 101–110). Abingdon, England: Routledge.

References

Adcock, C. J. (1965). Thematic Apperception Test. In O. Buros (Ed.), *The sixth mental measurement yearbook* (pp. 533–535). Highland Park, NJ: Gryphon Press.

Andersen, M. B. (Ed.). (2005). *Sport psychology in practice*. Champaign, IL: Human Kinetics.

Andersen, M. B., Barney, S. T., & Waterson, A. K. (2016). Mindfully dynamic meta-supervision: The case of AW and M. In J. G. Cremades & L. S. Tashman (Eds.), *Global practices and training in applied sport, exercise, and performance psychology: A case study approach* (pp. 330–342). New York, NY: Taylor & Francis.

Anzieu, D. (1960). *Les méthodes projectives*. Paris, France: P.U.F.

Apitzsch, E. (1995). Psychodynamic theory of personality and sport performance. In S. J. H. Biddle (Ed.), *European perspectives on exercise and sport psychology* (pp. 111–127). Champaign, IL: Human Kinetics.

Benzi, M., & Michelini, L. (1987). Psychological aspects of a group of national team artistic roller skaters. *Medicina Dello Sport, 40*, 419–422.

Cox, R. H. (2007). *Sport psychology: Concepts and applications* (6th ed.). New York, NY: WCB/McGraw-Hill.

Cratty, B. J. (1989). *Psychology in contemporary sport* (3rd ed.). Englewood Cliffs, NJ: Prentice-Hall.

Eron, L. D. (1959). Thematic Apperception Test. In O. Buros (Ed.), *The fifth mental measurements yearbook* (pp. 306–310). Highland Park, NJ: Gryphon Press.

Freud, S. (1953). Further remarks on the neuro-psychoses of defence. In J. Strachey (Trans. & Ed.), *The standard edition of the complete psychological works of Sigmund Freud* (Vol. III, pp. 157–185). London, England: Hogarth Press. (Original work published 1896.)

Jensen, A. R. (1959). Thematic Apperception Test. In O. Buros (Ed.), *The fifth mental measurements yearbook* (pp. 310–313). Highland Park, NJ: Gryphon Press.

Johnson, W. R., Hutton, D. C., & Johnson, G. B. (1954). Personality traits of some champion athletes as measured by two projective tests: Rorschach and H-T-P. *Research Quarterly, 25*, 484–485.

Killian, G. A., & Campbell, B. M. (1992). Object Relations Technique. In D. J. Keyser & R. C. Sweetland (Eds.), *Test critiques* (Vol. IX, pp. 469–477). Austin, TX: PRO-ED.

Lazarus, A. A. (1989). *The practice of multimodal therapy*. Baltimore, MD: Johns Hopkins University Press.
Morgan, C. D., & Murray, H. A. (1935). A method for investigating fantasies: The Thematic Apperception Test. *Archives of Neurology and Psychiatry*, *34*, 289–306. doi:10.1001/archneurpsyc.1935.02250200049005
Murray, H. A. (1938). *Explorations in personality: A clinical and experimental study of fifty men of college age*. New York, NY: Oxford University Press.
Rabin, A. I. (1986). Concerning projective techniques. In A. I. Rabin (Ed.), *Projective techniques for adolescents and children* (pp. 3–11). New York, NY: Springer.
Rorschach, H. (1921). *Psychodiagnostik*. Bern, Switzerland: Bircher.
Rotter, J. B. (1946). Thematic Apperception Tests: Suggestions for administration and interpretation. *Journal of Personality*, *15*, 70–92. doi:10.1111/j.1467-6494.1946.tb01052.x
Strean, W. B., & Strean, H. S. (1998). Applying psychodynamic concepts to sport psychology practice. *The Sport Psychologist*, *12*, 208–222. doi:10.1123/tsp.12.2.208

2 Development of the Athlete Apperception Technique[1]

The relationship between personality and sport participation has been a focus of researchers since the early work of sport psychology pioneer Coleman Griffith. Although the field of sport psychology, nowadays, is relatively diverse, sport psychological tools that measure personality-like traits (e.g., competitive trait anxiety, mental toughness) remain almost exclusively quantitative in design and format (e.g., scores on self-report pencil and paper tests usually with Likert-type scales). To our knowledge, and despite the growth of sport psychology as an established field of psychological endeavour, no projective technique has been fully developed for use with a sporting population. There is, however, a small and limited research trail of our previous work on the instrument described in this chapter, which includes the unpublished doctoral dissertation of the first author (Gibbs, 2006); a short, 3-page synopsis of the development of the AAT in the conference proceedings of the International Society of Sport Psychology (Gibbs, Marchant, & Andersen, 2005); a description of the AAT in a book chapter (Gibbs, 2010); and the article cited in note 1 (p. 47).

There is considerable support in sport psychology toward using divergent forms of personality assessment (Andersen, 2000, 2005; Conroy & Benjamin, 2001; Giges, 2000; Hill, 2001). Although many sport psychologists are trained and practice from a cognitive-behaviour model and prefer quantitative measures of assessment, we believe a need exists to introduce a *sport-themed* projective technique for those researchers and practitioners with interpersonal, depth psychology, and psychodynamic orientations. For example, the storytelling features of projective instruments such as the Thematic Apperception Test (TAT; Morgan & Murray, 1935) might add depth and nuances to the data gathered in case study and life history interview-based research.

Before proceeding further, we provide our rationale for the specific benefits of developing a sport-specific, storytelling, projective technique. First, the history of psychological assessment has largely been developed in the context of two potentially complementary, but sometimes viewed as opposing assessment paradigms: quantitative and qualitative (e.g., projective) testing. In contrast, the field of sport and exercise psychology has been almost entirely reliant on quantitative assessments. We believe the development of the Athlete Apperception Technique (AAT), and other psychodynamically based tools, will broaden the sport psychology assessment repertoire and provide a much-needed balance and depth. Second, there is an established history of domain-specific apperception techniques having been developed with the intent of better capturing the needs, values, motivations, attitudes, and unconscious conflicts and desires of specific populations. Two of the better-known derivative instruments are the Children's Apperception Test (Bellak & Bellak, 1949) and the Senior Apperception Technique (Bellak & Bellak, 1973). Although the original TAT has proven remarkably adaptable, we believe a sport-specific apperception instrument is needed. We expect that using a selection of contemporary sport images capable of tapping or *pulling* relevant themes including performance issues (e.g., anxiety, confidence, motivation, unconscious drivers); relationships (e.g., with coaches, parents, team-mates); self-concepts (e.g., core shame, worthiness); leadership; and team dynamics has substantial and widespread possibilities, especially for applied sport psychologists. Third, there are potential benefits of projective techniques as instruments for clinicians to identify manifest and latent issues, ego-defensive mechanisms, internal conflicts, unconscious motivations, and resistances that are difficult to access using quantitative measures. We believe a sport-specific apperception instrument can provide in-depth material for applied sport psychologists who are seeking to work dynamically and holistically with athletes. Fourth, that in our preliminary experiences using the AAT with athletes, there was a readiness to engage with the stimulus image material, and it seemed the athletes found the process interesting, and they appeared engaged in producing their stories.

In this chapter, we present three sequential studies by reporting on the stages of developing the AAT from conceptualisation to completion (a workable projective image set). We have taken inspiration from two specific sources. First, we went back to the pioneering work of Morgan and Murray (1935), who developed the original TAT. Second, we examined the unfulfilled promise of Bouet (1970) and Missoum and Laforestrie (1985), who independently attempted to develop sport apperception techniques. Their efforts, however, did not culminate in published or widely recognised sets of usable images. First, we briefly review the key features and methods of projective methods and techniques in general and the TAT in particular. Second, we discuss the relevance and use of apperception techniques in sport. Third, we outline the processes used to identify potentially suitable images for use in the final AAT image set. Fourth, we present Step 1, whereby we cull the set of images from 72 images (Set A) to 48 (Set B). Fifth, we describe Step 2 and the use of expert assessments of images to further reduce the number of potentially suitable images to 27 (Set C). Sixth, we describe the final step and the refinement to a set of 10 images (Set D – the AAT Image Set), a set of 5 supplementary images (AAT-S; Athlete Apperception Technique – Supplementary), and a set of 6 images for use with children (AAT-C: Athlete Apperception Technique – Children).

Projective techniques and the TAT

The rationale for the use of projective techniques is the psychodynamically based hypothesis that when confronted with ambiguous stimuli (e.g., inkblots, enigmatic images) and asked to explain what is going on in the picture, that individuals will place some structure on the stimuli and unconsciously project onto the image their own hopes, dreams, anxieties, desires, fears, and life stories. Projective techniques, historically referred to as *tests*, come in a variety of forms beyond inkblots and evocative images. There are word association tests, draw-a-person tests, sentence completion tests, and so forth, but they all rely on the process of projecting internal material on to whatever task is at hand.

There have been robust debates relating to projective techniques. For example, Lilienfeld, Wood, and Garb (2000) were critical of projective techniques especially about perceived shortcomings in reliability and validity. Hibbard (2003) responded with counter arguments that Lilienfeld et al. made errors of omission and commission. We are mindful that psychological assessment is broadly divided between quantitative assessment and qualitative/projective assessment traditions. The fundamental differences in these approaches have recently been neatly captured by Basu (2014),

> one [quantitative approach], aspiring to attain a structured and organized view of human behavior facilitating prediction, and the other [projective], an acceptance and appreciation of idiographic and divergent responses that may not necessarily be predictive, but informative about multiple possibilities of human thought process.
>
> (p. 25)

The TAT

The Thematic Apperception Test (TAT; Morgan & Murray, 1935) is used to stimulate people to tell stories that reveal their personal qualities, needs, desires, beliefs, and attitudes. Jenkins (2007) succinctly dignified the contribution of the TAT by stating, "the TAT has a long, honorable, and well-argued 65-year history in psychological research and clinical assessment" (p. 3).

The majority of the original 30 TAT images depict people in various life situations. Clients interpret the scene depicted, identify the central (main) character, explain what is taking place, describe the thoughts and feelings of the characters, describe the preceding events, and speculate on likely outcomes. The clients project onto the images their own hopes, dreams, fears, frustrations, relationships, and so forth. Murray (1938) stated, "If the procedure had merely exposed conscious fantasies and remembered events it would have been useful enough, but it did more than this. It gave the experimenter excellent clues for the divination of unconscious thematic formations" (p. 534). Murray believed clients are largely unaware (when they tell their stories about the images) that they are essentially talking about themselves and that their conscious defences are bypassed.

Projective techniques in sport

Although projective techniques have rarely been mentioned in the sport psychology literature, a few researchers have attempted to develop sport-themed projective technique. Bouet (1970) described a preliminary and un-validated sport-specific version of the TAT, the Projective Sport Test (PST). Bouet advocated that sporting activities are in essence projective phenomena "always acted out in situations intensely experienced" (p. 747). Using Anzieu's (1960) clinical interpretation guidelines for projective instrument development, athletes were administered the PST in conjunction with the Rorschach Inkblot Test and three other drawing-based projective tests. Bouet's research collaborator assessed each participant using results from the Rorschach and an un-named drawing-based test, and Bouet assessed participants using their responses to the PST. According to Bouet, the PST appeared to "provide the means for a discovery of the internal attitudes that proceed from the depths of the subject's motivational system, and also a rediscovery of the system through those attitudes" (p. 751). On further exploration, it appears that the PST remained at that preliminary phase. Bouet's PST is referenced in the *Directory of Psychological Tests in Sport and Exercise Sciences* (Ostrow, 1998) and stands as the only psychodynamically themed test of the 314 tests listed. Bouet's test and administration material, however, are not available.

In a similar study, Missoum and Laforestrie (1985) developed the Projective Test for Sportspersons (PTS) as part of a psychological assessment battery adapted for sport participants. Missoum and Laforestrie administered the assessment battery to 164 male athletes and non-athletes in an attempt to investigate self-concept. Both the Bouet (1970) and Missoum and Laforestrie research were incomplete and neither drove research to the point of practical use for practitioners or significant journal or manual publications. Possibly, from the 1960s through the 1980s, the fledgling field of sport psychology, being almost entirely dominated by quantitative methods and cognitive-behavioural paradigms, was resistant to accepting psychodynamic assessment methods. Irrespective of the specific reasons, efforts to develop a sport-specific projective tool did not progress past preliminary stages. The current research was sparked by the dormant work of Bouet and Missoum and Laforestrie and extends their work into the development of a complete sport-specific projective technique.

At this point, we prefer to promote the AAT as an adjunct clinical technique for tapping sport psychology themes and issues rather than a test or inventory per se, and not as an instrument for quantitative inquiry. We expect that subsequent work will determine the extent to which reliability, validity, trustworthiness, and clinical utility in their many forms, pertain to the AAT.

General methods: image set development

Our intention was to broadly adhere to the instrument construction principles Morgan and Murray (1935) used in developing the TAT. Henry (1956) and Murray (1938, 1965) suggested a number of criteria for devising new image sets. According to Henry,

> the pictures should be drawn or selected as to employ persons, dress, object, background that are not thought to be inappropriate by the persons being studied . . . they need only be portrayed in a general manner so as to enable the subjects to feel that the persons could be people like them. (p. 51)

As with most derivatives of the TAT, the images used in the AAT were not originally designed specifically for projective use. Consistent with Murray's procedures (1943), a preliminary image set of 149 images was compiled from numerous sources (e.g., newspapers, magazines, web pages) that represented various styles of graphic design (e.g., photographs, pencil drawings, paintings). Much of the initial collection and reduction of the preliminary images took place under the supervision of Wesley Morgan (University of Tennessee), an expert in the history and selection of images for projective assessment, and particularly the history of TAT image sets (see Morgan, 2002). The initial bank of potential images was reduced through this expert consultation process from 149 images to 72 images in preparation for image Set A (Step 1).

Step 1: image Set A

For the first step in the AAT development, the sport corollary of the figures and relationships depicted in the TAT is coach–athlete, athlete–athlete, athlete–adversary, and a range of interpersonal relations (father–son, mother–daughter, siblings, peers). Image Set A consisted of 72 images representing a range of sport situations (e.g., solitary or team situations; peer or coach interactions; interpersonal relations; pre, during, and post sport events). We also deliberately included images of both positive and negative situations. Another purposeful intention was to include images that would evoke athletes' experiential knowledge of daily struggles in their chosen sports and interpersonal relations. A final, bedrock of projective techniques is image ambiguity, and we endeavoured to select images that lent themselves to multiple and differential interpretations. The general aim of this step was to reduce this image set by at least a third by assessing the written and verbal responses of athletes to these images.

Method

For the reduction of images in this first step, we used thematic content analysis, a process of recovering structures of meanings given by participants and represented in their written responses to the images (Teglasi, 2001). Thematic content analysis and theme counting methods have often been used to reduce large numbers of images into workable image sets. In particular, we adopted content import analysis, a specific thematic content analysis method for the treatment of projective response data. Consistent with recommended procedures (Teglasi, 2001) we began by "diagramming the underlying structure of the story content according to its key elements" (Teglasi, 2001, p. 53). Each story was broken down into five key elements: (a) the *circumstance*, akin to what is happening in the picture or what happened before; (b) the *intention* of the characters in the story, such as motives, goals, and feelings; (c) the *complication* facing the characters, such as anticipated or unexpected events and internal barriers or conflicts; (d) the *means* or actions and other coping strategies of characters; and (e) the *outcome*, that is, how things will turn out. Analysis of the content import requires at least some basic interpretation and is somewhat subjective.

Participants

All participants were athletes recruited from community sporting clubs or universities. Data collection consisted of administering images from Set A to 184 athletes (76 females, 108 males), ranging in age from 18 to 46 years.

Participants represented over 20 sports ranging in competition level from amateur to elite inclusive of 111 team sports participants and 73 individual sports participants. All participants completed standard informed consent procedures.

Procedures

Image Set A was administered using a variety of methods, including a self-administration and a group administration. Overall, we showed all 72 images to participants, but because of the number of images, each administration group received a different set of images. All participants received identical instructions for responding to the presented images including: interpret the scene depicted in the image, identify the central character, explain what is taking place, describe the thoughts and feelings of the characters, describe the preceding events, and speculate on a likely outcome. There were 93 participants in the self-administration group, who were provided with one of two sets of 18 images, response forms, and a return envelope. In the group administration, 91 participants attended three administration sessions held several days apart. Each participant responded to 12 images in each session (total of 36 images) with each image projected onto a screen while participants wrote brief stories.

Findings and discussion

Responses to all 72 images were thematically content analysed to identify images that elicited rich and varied responses and to help determine those images to be retained for image Set B; we had no set number of images in mind, but we were simply led by the results of the analysis. There were no evident differences in response style or length of stories between the participants who took their images home for 3 weeks (a return rate of 72%) and the individuals who attended the group administration data collection. Raw data were reduced using content import analysis. Participants produced short stories ranging in length from a couple of sentences (less than 25 words) to a small paragraph (50 or more words). Some images evoked detailed, protracted, and complex stories, and other images elicited uncomplicated and succinct stories. Following content import analysis, we used three specific criteria to reduce the image set: (a) parallel/overlapping, (b) sport–situation ambiguity, and (c) response size/complexity. For example, images that elicited responses paralleling other images, but with a smaller range of themes, were discarded. Similarly, images that stimulated responses whereby participants had difficulty in recognising the sport situation or evoked responses limited in size and/or complexity, were also discarded. Our eventual aim

Table 2.1 Content import analysis

Content Element	*Narrative*
Circumstance	Golfer trying to put the ball in hole
Intention	Not happy about missing and embarrassed
Complication	Upset with ball; he prepared but still missed
Means	Look to the ground, and then putt quickly
Outcome	Taps the ball into the hole

was to cull the image set to a workable size and then have these images redrawn as original sketches by a professional artist. For each of the images described here, we provide the original number assigned to that image and include a brief author description of what that image depicts. Participants were, however, simply shown a copy of the image and not the brief author description. We have included the analysis of responses to Image 01 (from the group administration). Image 01, like many of the original images used pre-Step 1 and in Step 1 and Step 2, was a photograph or illustration found during a web search for "sporting situations." (Note: for copyright reasons, we will show only the final version of AAT images in this text, e.g., the drawings created specifically for the AAT). Image 01 is described as a male golfer putting a golf ball; the ball appears to have "over-run" the hole.

The following is an example of how image responses were organised using content import analysis (see Table 2.1). An example of a typical story response to Image 01, and the subsequent basic content import analysis used during Step 1 analysis, follows:

> A golfer is the main character. He is trying to putt a golf ball into a hole. He would probably be pretty upset with the golf ball, and would not be happy it did not go in. The golfer would have prepared for the putt, focusing on hitting it in, before getting in his stance, and then putting. He will probably look down at the ground, embarrassed about missing the shot, then walk to the ball and quickly tap it in.

Import: If someone misses a goal they may have thought too much about it. Maybe external factors (e.g., the ball) or internal factors (e.g., over-preparation) are at blame. It is best not to think too much and simply focus on the job at hand.

Responses to all 72 images were thematically content analysed to determine images that elicited rich and varied responses. Raw data were reduced using content import analysis. Based on the stories of participants to Image 01, "A male golfer attempting a short putt" (see Table 2.2 for representative

Table 2.2 Image 01 representative participant quotes

Content Element	*Narrative*
Circumstance	"he is trying to get the ball in the hole" "golfer has teed off and has got the ball on the green" "just attempted a putt, which has subsequently missed" "I think this was an important shot to miss"
Intention	"embarrassed about missing the shot" "he could be disappointed if he misses" "he'll get angry he missed" "golfer is either feeling happy or sad getting the ball in hole"
Complication	"fantastic round of golf; now the pressure is on for final putt" "due to nerves he hit the ball too hard and overshot the hole" "golfer is in a tie breaker situation for the Australian PGA" "needs this putt to force a playoff"
Means	"he might talk to the ball because he wants it to go in" "looking at the shot and examining what he did wrong" "smash his club or swear or throw his head back in anger" "practiced the shot away from the ball, even visualising shot"
Outcome	"will get the ball in and go to next hole or finish/win game" "birdie the next three holes to a record personal best round" "will probably throw his fist in the air and look at the crowd" "miss the putt and be angry with himself and throw his putter"

participant quotes), the responses representing the *circumstance* content of the image included a male golfer attempting to get the ball in the hole, or a golfer about to miss or having already missed. The *intention* content of the image included the golfer contemplating his miss, feeling angry, frustrated or disappointed, embarrassed about missing, or feeling satisfied and confident. Responses representing the *complication* content included the central character (usually an adult male golfer) being under pressure to win the match, making a good shot, dealing with an intensely stressful situation, or dealing with a difficult hole (pin placement). The *means* content included the golfer visualising the club as an extension of his arm, getting upset with club and ball, acting out aggressively, or using techniques such as visualisation and pre-shot routines. Finally, responses to Image 01 representing the *outcome* content included the golfer winning the tournament/match, making the shot he needed, acknowledging the crowd and being celebrated as a champion, or losing and feeling disgrace and anger.

At the completion of the content import analysis, it was apparent that some images evoked parallel themes. For example, both Image 05 (a young male baseball player sits on bench – shoulders slumped forward – looking dejected or exhausted; a bag is under the bench) and Image 11 (a male athlete sits on a bench with his head in his hands and elbows on his knees – looking dejected or exhausted) evoked themes such as: losing an event; missing selection on a team; feeling pressure, disappointment, anger, or rejection; doubting ability; lacking support from others; sulking or avoidance; and retiring from sport. Image 05 evoked a broader range of themes than Image 11, such as disappointment or disapproval from an introduced figure (e.g., coach, team-mate, parent), and feeling depressed, and, accordingly, was retained in preference to Image 11.

All the images in Set A depicted sport situations and a variety of sport themes, but some images evoked responses that reflected some confusion as to the sport situation, or specific recognition of the sport itself. One criterion introduced by projective test experts is a degree of ambiguity, but not to the extent that the situation is unrecognisable. Two examples of ambiguity regarding the sport situation are evident in responses to Image 88 (several rowers carry their oars held high in the air like spears or poles) and Image 64 (several sets of synchronised swimmer's legs stick out of the pool surface). Image 88 evoked varied responses such as a group of people practicing pole-vaulting, pole-vaulters preparing for competition, or male warriors going to battle. Image 64 evoked common responses such as synchronised swimmers practicing or competing. Image 88 was retained for Set B because the image evoked stories with varying themes and some ambiguity, especially what the group of people were attempting (e.g., athletes practicing or competing, warriors preparing or in battle). Conversely, Image 64 was not retained because the sport and sport situation were specifically well defined, and participant stories produced very little ambiguity and variation.

An example of excessive ambiguity was noticeable in responses to Image 71 (several females, maybe runners, collapsed on the floor in distress; being covered by blankets) and Image 07 (an adult male sits next to a young male with a fishing pole on the edge of a body of water). Image 71 evoked responses such as complete exhaustion, busy ambulance workers, competitors cooling down, or distressed supporters. There was also confusion as to the sport being played (e.g., "can't make out what is happening," "what has this got to do with sport?"). Image 07 evoked responses such as a boy and father fishing and talking about life, a father and son moment, and a father comforting his son. Again, there was confusion as to why this image was included in a sport-themed set (e.g., "just two people talking, nothing else going on," "is fishing a sport?"). Both Image 71 and Image 07 were considered too ambiguous to be retained for Set B.

Some Set A images evoked responses that were limited in size (word count) and complexity. An example of images at either end of the response *size* continuum were Image 14 (a male coach talks to a young male American football player [in a helmet]) and Image 99 (a track and field relay baton-change between a white runner and a black runner). We used the word count method only in the early stage of image set reduction primarily as an approximate guide. Word count assisted in comparing similar images that evoked like themes but with varying lengths of stories. Participants created stories in response to Image 14 that were substantial in size (an average of 62 words per story) compared to stories in response to Image 99 (averaging only 22 words per story). Image 14 usually evoked responses such as a coach comforting a player, a coach and player with a close relationship, a player disappointed with his performance and a coach giving reassurance, an important match, a player who has failed, a player looking unhappy or angry due to a poor performance, or a coach trying to encourage and motivate a player. Image 99 generally evoked responses such as two male athletes passing a baton, one of the men dropping the baton, and celebration or disappointment at the end of the race. A low word count average was an indication that images were not evoking rich and varied stories compared to images with a high word count averages such as Image 14.

An example of images residing at either end of the response *complexity* continuum were Image 60 (two female hurdlers, one successful negotiating a hurdle, the other approaching a hurdle apprehensively) and Image 10 (a drawing of three young girls playing). Responses to Image 60 generally reflected the intensity of the situation and the inner-voices or self-talk of the athletes. Image 60 evoked stories such as competitors struggling to make it over the hurdles, a girl trying to catch up and pushing herself, thoughts of hopelessness and fear, thoughts of determination and dedication, respect for each other as competitors, and elation or disappointment in the outcome. Image 10 evoked responses such as: girls in a running race, a sports day at school, girls running with smiles on their faces, high spirits, and kids having fun. Image 60 is an example of an image that evoked rich, complex stories that participants related to emotionally and was retained for use in Set B, whereas Image 10 evoked relatively meagre stories and was discarded.

Many responses to Image 10 also focused on the creation of the image rather than the content (e.g., "picture probably drawn by a young child," "cartoon picture of girls running," "a little kid's drawing"). There were a variety of artistic media used throughout image Set A, for example, photographs, paintings, and drawings. Many of the photographs were also graphically manipulated and distorted to disguise the athletes depicted, and for copyright reasons. The initial reason for using a variety of media was to produce a more varied and visually stimulating image set. One drawback of that approach was reflected in participants' stories to several images, such as Image 10, where the story was more focused on the style of image (e.g., cartoon, distorted picture) than the situation depicted. All cartoon-style images were discarded, but other images that evoked description of the medium (e.g., distorted picture, painting), and also evoked rich and varied stories, were retained for use in Set B.

As a result of this content import analysis, theme counting, and comparison of average responses, image Set A was reduced from 72 images to 48 images (Set B) for further assessment. The images retained evoked succinct and varied responses, produced distinct themes, were visually appealing and resulted in responses that clearly identified the sports and sport situations. We were satisfied that Step 1 was useful in helping to identify sport-specific images representative of the central factors that Murray (1943) identified (viz., comprehensiveness, ambiguity, complexity, identification, and stimulating power). We were mindful, particularly in the context of previous unfulfilled efforts, that further research was needed in working toward producing an image set of a manageable size.

Step 2: the input of experts on image Set B

In aiming to refine and improve the AAT, we engaged experts to assess image suitability and content import. Several researchers (e.g., Cronbach, 1990; Lynn, 1986) have commented on the composition of expert panels, including the number of judges required. Lynn recommended, on statistical grounds, "that a minimum of five judges should provide a sufficient level of control for chance agreement" (p. 383). From a practical standpoint, the number of judges making up an expert panel is largely dictated by the availability and willingness of experts to participate in the assessment process. It was, however, apparent that in sport psychology there are few experts in projective technique development. The intended outcome was to reduce image Set B (48 images) to a smaller set (Set C) using expert judgement. The 12 participants, hereafter referred to as *judges*, were instructed to rate the appropriateness and content of 48 images using five specific criteria representative of the central factors that Murray (1943) identified with the TAT (ambiguity, identification, latent stimulus, interpersonal relations, and qualities that stimulate creative faculties).

A further goal of Step 2 was to investigate and assess item content validity. Authors of *The Standards for Educational and Psychological Testing* assert that "content related evidence . . . is a central concern during test development" (American Educational Research Association, 1999, p. 11). There remains a longstanding debate among psychometricians (e.g., Cronbach, 1990; Haynes, Richard, & Kubany, 1995; Messick, 1975, 1989) as to whether the term *content validity* should be used to describe judges' content ratings. According to Dunn, Bouffard, and Rogers (1999), regardless of the label used, the assessment of content validity is a crucial validation process. The use of expert judges in the image assessment procedure was central to the content-related validation process. Content validity evidence may include information relating to both the content-relevance of individual items and the content representativeness of the item set. Cronbach (1990) suggested that many researchers tend to under-report or under-value the assessment of item (analogous to image) content-relevance. Validity is defined as the degree that the test accomplishes the purpose for which it is being used (Mehrens & Lehmann, 1987; Worthen, Borg, & White, 1993). Content validity refers to the extent that test items represent the entire body of content to be assessed or measured. According to Worthen et al., content representativeness is whether the questions adequately represent the universe of possible questions. For the AAT, establishing evidence of image relevance and representativeness of the target domain was an important step in validating images.

Step 2 is mostly a quantitative analysis of image ratings, however, there remains a purposeful qualitative component in the process of reducing the image set. One limitation of the present step is the unnatural fit between the language used in qualitative work and traditional psychometric terminology (e.g., applied to quantitative tests). There is a question of the appropriateness in using psychometric terminology when discussing projective technique development; nevertheless, this was one step of many used to identify the images most suitable for inclusion in the final image set.

Method

The experts

The participant experts were recruited at an annual meeting of the Australian College of Clinical Psychologists (ACCP). These 12 participants (2 female 10 male) ranged in age from 25 to 54 years. All participants had completed either master's degree (5) or doctoral degree (7) in clinical, counselling, or sport psychology. Participants (judges) were asked about their experience in personality assessment, especially projective assessment. Seven judges considered themselves well versed in the administration and interpretation of projective techniques. The sport psychologists, with some or little experience with projective techniques, were also included as judges because we considered them to have familiarity with the population for whom the instrument was intended (Crocker & Algina, 1986), and their insights into behaviours in sport contexts were valuable additions to the contributions of the clinical psychologists.

Procedures

Following an informal presentation during the ACCP conference, we asked for volunteer participants. Those who were interested in taking part completed informed consent procedures. We then provided each judge with a package that included all materials necessary to rate images and some background literature on the rating criteria. Cronbach (1990) suggested that "expert raters" should be provided with as much information as possible to make informed judgements on the adequacy of instrument construction and validation processes. Judges need clear instructions on the rating process, including item-evaluation or item-rating procedures (Dunn et al., 1999). Judges are often asked to rate items (or in this case, images) on a 5-point Likert-type rating scale such as 1 (*very poor fit*) to 5 (*excellent fit*). Likert scales are popular because they provide test developers with both quantified item ratings, as well as the opportunity to evaluate and summarise judgements using statistical procedures.

We asked the judges to familiarise themselves with the domain specifications and instructed them to study the 48 images, and rate each image on a 5-point scale using the following five criteria: (a) *image ambiguity*, (b) *evoke identification*, (c) *latent stimulus*, (d) *interpersonal relations*, and (e) *creative faculties*. The instructions to "judges" were:

1. *Ambiguity in image*. Each image should be ambiguous enough that participants have room to create stories that reflect their own internal and external worlds. During the development of the Thematic Apperception Test (TAT), Murray (1943) found that there was a tendency at first to select images that told too much. Many of the images elicited very similar stories and responses from participants, and Murray believed that participants had to be given more scope to create stories that reflected their own internal and external worlds.
2. *The image should evoke identification*. Murray (1943) considered it preferable that there should be at least one person in each image with whom the client (participant) could easily identify. The term identification, used in reference to the projective character of the TAT, may be confusing because it usually refers to the process of putting oneself in the position of another. In connection with the TAT, Murray suggested identification refers to, "a process whereby a story-teller feels or imagines himself inside a character he is creating (rather than looking at the character from the outside), and thus, gets into a relationship with this character which is similar (inside, close, intimate) to the relationship that he has with his own psyche" (Anderson, 1999, p. 32).
3. *Each image must have a potent latent stimulus meaning*. "Existing in hidden form, dormant but capable of being evoked or developed. Often in psychoanalytic theory an infant's ego processes are said to be latent; in cognitive psychology particular intellectual processes that have not yet manifested themselves are referred to as latent; and so forth" (Reber, 1995, p. 408).
4. Several images should depict *basic interpersonal relations* (e.g., various family dyads such as mother–child, father–child, sibling; a person

alone; two persons of the same age and sex; persons in varying social roles). There should be enough information in the images to stimulate a substantial variety of stories about different relationship configurations or qualities (Sherwood, 1957). For the purpose of the present study, the sport corollary may be mother–child, father–child, coach–athlete, athlete–athlete, athlete–adversary, and so forth.

5. *Images should encourage exercise of imaginative and creative faculties.* "Each picture . . . while it tends to evoke associations bearing upon a particular topic or theme, its content and the situation it suggests will be incomplete to a degree that the subject . . . will be obliged to exercise imaginative and creative faculties" (Sherwood, 1957, p. 173).

The 5-point Likert scale used by judges included the following instructions: 1 (*not a hint*), 2 (*not much*), 3 (*some*), 4 (*a lot*), and 5 (*abundant*) (see Table 2.3). Judges also were given instructions to rate images as stand-alone depictions of sporting situations, and *not* on suitability as a part of a complete thematic image set for the purpose of this research. They were also told that following their expert ratings (and subsequent analysis), selected images would be used to finalise an image set appropriate for use in a sport-themed projective technique.

Judges rated individual images in Step 2 and then had no further part in the development of the AAT. According to Dunn et al. (1999), the assessment of content should be conducted by individuals who are not involved in the original development of the test-construction process. Dunn et al. suggested such individuals will almost certainly be biased in their assessment due to preconceived notions.

Table 2.3 Image assessment form

Image	*Image Ambiguity*	*Evoke Identification*	*Latent Stimulus*	*Interpersonal Relations*	*Creative Facilities*
#01	*not a hint* 1	*not a hint* 1	*not a hint* 1	*not a hint* 1	*not a hint* 1
A male golfer missing a putt	*not much* 2	*not much* 2	*not much* 2	*not much* 2	*not much* 2
	some 3	*some* 3	*some* 3	*some* 3	*some* 3
	a lot 4	*a lot* 4	*a lot* 4	*a lot* 4	*a lot* 4
	abundant 5	*abundant* 5	*abundant* 5	*abundant* 5	*abundant* 5

Findings

In the construction of a qualitative instrument, the use of basic quantitative methods (e.g., means and standard deviations) can have heuristic value in making determinations of when experts ratings indicate that an image is of questionable value or likely to be of use and should be included in the refined projective technique. Judges' ratings were an integral process in the overall image set reduction in this step. For an image to be considered acceptable, we established specific standards: $M > 3.50$ and $SD < 1.00$ on at least three of the five criteria. High mean ratings and low standard deviations provide evidence regarding the degree that images are content-relevant. For example, using the first criterion (i.e., ambiguity), an $M > 3.50$ indicates there is a medium to high level of ambiguity of the image. Conversely, an $M < 2.50$ indicates little ambiguity, and a $SD < 1.00$ indicates some consensus among judges on their ratings.

The first criterion used in the validation process was *image ambiguity*. According to Murray (1943), each image should be ambiguous enough that participants have room to create stories that reflect their own internal and external worlds. As a result of the rating process, 21 images appeared to have medium-to-high levels of ambiguity. The second criterion was *evoke identification*. From the experts' ratings, 9 images had a medium-to-high likelihood of evoking identification. The third criterion was *latent stimulus*. Images must have a potent latent stimulus meaning; essentially, dormant feelings should be evoked. There were 22 images that had a medium-to-high likelihood of evoking stories with potent latent stimulus meanings. The fourth criterion was *interpersonal relations*. Several images depicted dyads such as mother–child, father–child, coach–athlete, athlete–athlete, and athlete–adversary. We found 15 images to have a medium-to-high likelihood of evoking stories about interpersonal relations. The fifth criterion was *creative faculties*, whereby images should lend themselves to exercising imaginative and creative faculties. For this criterion, 25 images had a medium-to-high likelihood of stimulating imaginative and creative faculties.

Included in Tables 2.4 and 2.5, the frequency and descriptive statistics for judges' ratings of two images are included as an example. The overall highest ranked image was Image 73 (an adult female comforts a younger female in an embrace). Image 73 met the established means and standard deviations in all five of the set criteria (see Table 2.4). High mean ratings and low standard deviations provide initial evidence regarding the degree that the images can be considered content-relevant (Dunn et al., 1999). The lowest overall ranked image was Image 76 (a female bodybuilder poses in an open-gender competition) and this image did not meet the jointly established standards (M and SD) for any of the five criteria (see Table 2.5). The high standard

Table 2.4 Judges' ratings of Image 73

Criterion	*None*	*Not much*	*Some*	*A lot*	*Abundant*	*M*	*SD*
image ambiguity	0	0	5	6	1	3.67	0.65
evoke identification	0	0	2	9	1	3.92	0.51
latent stimulus	0	0	2	8	2	4.00	0.60
interpersonal relations	0	0	0	3	9	4.75	0.45
creative faculties	0	0	1	8	3	4.12	0.58

Table 2.5 Judges' ratings of Image 76

Criterion	*None*	*Not much*	*Some*	*A lot*	*Abundant*	*M*	*SD*
image ambiguity	1	3	4	2	2	3.80	1.80
evoke identification	2	4	2	4	0	3.08	1.24
latent stimulus	0	3	3	4	2	3.42	1.08
interpersonal relations	0	6	4	1	1	2.75	0.97
creative faculties	0	5	2	3	2	3.12	1.19

deviations for most of the criteria were the major assessment concern for this image and other images with similarly high variability and lack of consensus.

Based on the judges' ratings, 27 images were considered as likely to evoke rich and varied stories in at least three of the criteria. The remaining 21 images were discarded because they rated high in less than three of the five criteria.

Each image in Set B was individually analysed to assess strengths and weaknesses according to the judges' ratings. A further investigation of the average ratings of the entire image set provided additional evidence for the removal of particular images from Set B. For example, the average rating of all 48 images for the image ambiguity criterion was $M = 3.38$, with a $SD = 0.87$, and the average rating of a reduced 27 image set (Set C) for image ambiguity was $M = 3.71$, with a $SD = 0.79$. The reduced image Set C (27 images) had higher means and lower standard deviations for each of the five criteria than image Set B (48 images).

By reducing the set, we had clear evidence that the level of ambiguity and the range of responses had increased. Those images that did not evoke a reasonably strong response for the five criteria assessed were discarded. This process follows the logic of quantitative test construction research in that weaker, and overlapping items (images) are removed. We believe that the expert rating procedure was a successful step in the overall process of reducing the image set to a workable size.

Step 3: reducing image Set C to a final product (Set D)

For Step 3, we used two interpretive methods for the analyses of images, one a relatively new method and the other, a standard in projective test literature. The first method, developed by Teglasi (2001), is a popular interpretive strategy. We recast the details of a projective story into abstract themes, constituting the moral of the story. Abstract themes, a moral for each story, and a sound understanding of content support the second method of analysis used in this study. The second method was based on a traditional projective story interpretation that Henry (1956) developed with the focus being on identifying the *stimulus properties* of the image. Henry suggested that the interpretation of images requires the examiner to acquire knowledge of several categories of analysis in which the images may be described. Listed below are the six categories of analysis Henry outlined:

I. *Artist's description* – A brief description of the image.

II. *Manifest stimulus demand (of the image)* – Manifest aspects are usually observed by respondents and used in their stories. There are certain aspects of the story that may be considered as *given* or represent *avoidance*, *misinterpretation*, or *distortion*. Careful consideration should be used in deciding what is *given* and what may be a distortion with special interpretive significance. There are three categories of manifest stimulus demand:

   (a) *Adequate stimulus notation* refers to the major segments of the stimulus frequently used by respondents to build a story.
   (b) *Other details often noted* refer to frequently observed details not referred to in the plot.
   (c) *Seldom noted details* refer to details observed by a small percentage of respondents.

III. *Form demand* – Images differ in the form pattern presented to the respondent and likely reflect varying degrees of task difficulty.

IV. *Latent stimulus demand* – The latent stimulus is typically presented as an underlying emotional issue.

V. *Frequent plots* – Refers to the usual manner that respondents integrate the previous features and the story development.

VI. *Significant variations* – There are some variations of response that should be closely examined and may require further clarification.

Henry's (1956) interpretive methods, used to assist in the development of the AAT, have been widely used in other projective tests/techniques.

Method

Participants

A group administration was conducted with 75 university students (36 females, 39 males), age range 17–35 years. Overall, 21 sports were represented with 41 participants playing team sports, and 34 playing individual sports. The five most represented sports were: Australian football (14), track and field (8), basketball (7), netball (6), and tennis (4). Participants ranged in competition level from amateurs to elite athletes. Standard informed consent procedures were used, and the participants were different from those used in Steps 1 and 2.

Procedure

The proposed image Set C of 27 photographs and drawings was sent to a professional artist who, once briefed with specifications for each image, created original sketches. We chose an artist who was able to redraw the photographs using a consistent and original style (Kerri Gibbs, New York, NY). The redrawn images of Set C were administered to participants over three sessions spaced 1 week apart. During each of the three sessions, participants were given 75 minutes to develop and compose nine stories. We instructed participants to write a short story about each image that included identifying the central character, describing the central character's thoughts and emotions, suggesting what the central character is doing, explaining what is happening in the scene, describing what led to this moment, and suggesting a likely outcome.

Findings

First, a content import analysis based on the written stories of participants was used to examine responses. Second, descriptions of the stimuli (stimulus properties) of each image was developed based on the content import of responses and identification of prominent themes for each image. We also chose to investigate and identify gender response variations. Henry's (1956) and Teglasi's (2001) story analysis methods were influential in developing a clear and detailed description of the stimulus properties for each image (see Chapter 3).

The first step in the analysis was to transcribe 2,025 stories (75 participants × 27 stories), resulting in a data set containing over 130,000 words. Participants produced short stories ranging in length from a few sentences (less than 40 words) to a paragraph (up to 120 words). The majority of images evoked detailed and complex stories, although some images evoked more thematically diverse responses than others. Participants' stories for each image were divided by gender and analysed for content and major themes. The content import summaries are representative of the written responses of all participants. Overall, for males and females, there were few differences in responses to images. Male and female quantitative responses are reported as grouped together, but we have included additional comments regarding differences where noteworthy.

Image stimulus properties

The stimulus properties are summary descriptions of both the content imports and quantitative responses of participants to each image. The stimulus properties also include identification of prominent sport psychology themes and brief gender response variations where applicable. Below is an example of the stimulus properties of Image 02 (see Table 2.6). The stimulus properties for all AAT images is presented in Chapter 3.

I. *Artist's description.* A male athlete lying on a running track.
II. *Manifest stimulus demand (of the image).* The usual account of this image includes a reference to the athlete lying on the track and some description of how the athlete progressed to that position. Other details often noted are having collapsed and issues of coping and responses to injury.
III. *Form demand.* The form of this image involves the athlete and why he is lying on the track.
IV. *Latent stimulus demand.* Image 02 primarily relates to general issues of despair versus elation, and the relationship of personal demands to those of outside agents (e.g., coach, team-mates, crowd). Personal concepts of intrinsic and extrinsic motivation may be revealed.
V. *Frequent plots.* The basic plots to this image are: (a) runner falls to the ground before the end of the race and is distraught, (b) runner falls to ground after winning the race and is elated, (c) runner falls due to an injury but gets up and courageously finishes the race, (d) runner falls due to an injury and remains on the track in despair.

Table 2.6 Image 02 stimulus properties

	Image	*Psychosocial and Performance Themes (PPT)* *Latent Stimulus Demand Summary (LSDS)*
02		PPT: responses to injury, intrinsic/extrinsic motivation, confidence LSDS: despair versus elation, relationship of personal demands to those of outside agents, familiarity of negative emotions, attributional style, passive or assertive nature of personal defences

VI. *Significant variations.* Any deviation from the preceding may be a significant variation, including any introduced figure, most frequently the coach, the crowd, or parent and the figure's relationship to any of the above.

VII. *Gender Variations.* One major variation is the manner in which the issue of despair or elation is handled, particularly at the end of the story. Females are more likely to describe a mechanical method to recovery and handling of elation or despair (e.g., catch breath, enjoy the moment) and the outcome (e.g., will get up and try again, will rest before attempting again). Males are more likely to describe an outcome that is grandiose (e.g., wins gold medal, acknowledges the roaring crowd).

Reduction of image Set C

The reduction of image Set C involved considering and comparing themes and the latent stimulus demand of images. The following is a brief comparison and discussion of image stimulus properties' characteristics and the rationale for retaining or discarding specific Set C images. Most Set C images evoked distinct themes and appeared to have well-defined stimulus properties. For each image, a clear primary psychosocial sport theme emerged along with secondary themes in some cases. The majority of images produced themes of general interpersonal relations and athletic identity. Where appropriate, we noted specific aspects of interpersonal relations (i.e., father–son, father–daughter, mother–daughter, siblings, peers, competitors, coach–athlete). Images with similar psychosocial sport themes were compared, and the image with more variability in primary and secondary themes was chosen over the less variable image.

There were instances where two images evoked identical themes, but in some of those instances, we retained both images because they had distinct latent stimulus properties. Several images produced similar themes and similar stimulus properties. For example, Image 02 (a male athlete lying on a running track), Image 05 (a young male baseball player sits on bench; a bag is under the bench), Image 26 (a young female softball player sits on grass next to base, with head in hand), and Image 32 (an exhausted young male sits on a chair with shirt off and eyes closed) all evoked the themes of losing an event, missing selection on a team, perceived pressure, disappointment, anger, frustration, rejection, having doubts about ability, lacking support from others, lacking motivation, sulking or avoidance, incurring an injury, and retiring from sport. Image 02 and Image 05 did, however, evoke a broader range of themes than Image 26 and Image 32. Essentially, Image 02 and Image 05 evoked more emotionally complex stories than Image 26 and Image 32, as well as eliciting a wider range of psychosocial themes. Accordingly, Image 02 and Image 05 were retained in preference to Image 26 and Image 32.

Through the use of a multi-method approach to analysis, image Set C was reduced by determining and retaining those images that evoked the richest and most varied responses. The final set was determined using a combination of theme identification, content import analysis, thematic analysis, and stimulus properties comparisons, focusing on a complete image set that evoked a wide range of psychosocial themes and latent stimulus properties. Overall, 10 images were identified as suitable for inclusion in the final (Set D) image set. The numbers of the images were changed and ordered from 1 through to 10 to create the final, and present AAT Image Set (see Figure 2.1). The

Figure 2.1 AAT image set

sport psychology themes and the stimulus properties of each AAT image are presented in Chapter 3.

The supplemental images (AAT-S)

We rejected many images to make up the final AAT image set, but several of the discarded images had properties or evoked themes that may identify the presence of specific dispositions or complexes. As a result of Step 3, we finalised three image sets: (a) the core image set (AAT), (b) a supplementary set (AAT-S), and (c) a children's set (AAT-C). The AAT-S (see Figure 2.2) comprises five images that also evoke a range of sport psychology themes and latent stimulus properties. The AAT-S, however, is best viewed as an optional set for practitioners who are intentionally pursuing particular sport situations and sport themes they believe are useful when working with particular clients. Those sport psychology themes (SPT) and latent stimulus demand (LSD) themes include vulnerability, conflict and arousal and authority consequences, attitudes toward faith in a sport setting, gay male issues, dependency and passivity towards superior uncontrollable forces, apprehension over body contact, attitudes of personal activity/passivity, jealously, gloating, and boasting. The sport psychology themes and the stimulus properties of each AAT-S image are presented in Chapter 3.

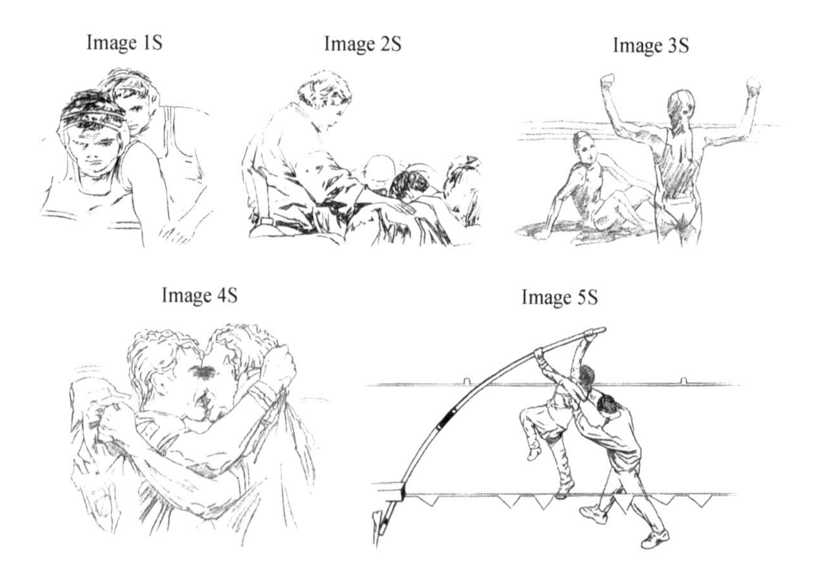

Figure 2.2 AAT-S image set

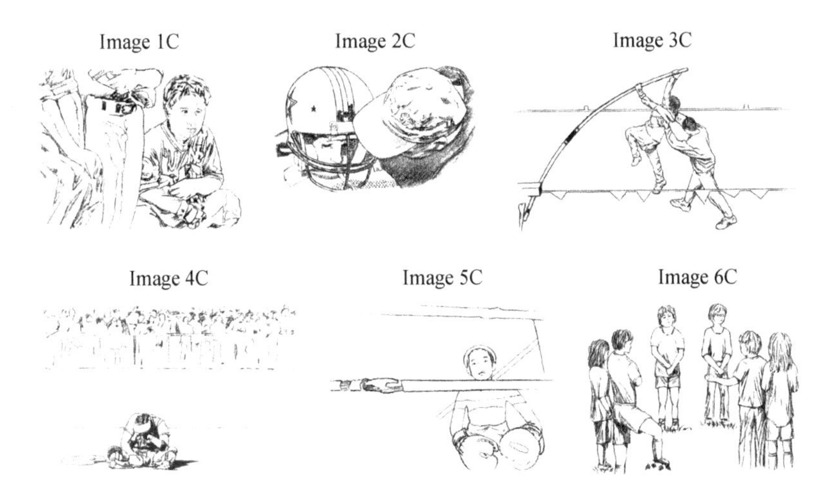

Figure 2.3 AAT-C image set

The children's images (AAT-C)

The AAT Children's set (AAT-C; see Figure 2.3) includes 6 images and is made up of a small subset of the original AAT 10 images (nos. 2 and 6), one of the AAT-S: Supplementary images (no. 5S), plus 3 new images. The contents of these images may help children easily identify with the character portrayed and are likely to evoke stories reflecting child- and adolescent-relevant issues such as sport development and barriers to sport involvement. The AAT-C has not been administered as an image set to children and no further information has been collected other than what has been presented up to this point. We present this set as a suggestion only and recommend that the validity and utility of the AAT-C should be examined further. The sport psychology themes and the stimulus properties of each AAT-C image are presented in Chapter 3.

Discussion

The development of the AAT accords with the recent trend in projective technique construction of developing population-specific instruments that include domain-specific scenes in image sets (e.g., athletes in sport settings). In constructing the AAT, we have followed the developmental model used to construct the TAT (Morgan & Murray, 1935). As discussed, an important element in the development of projective techniques is creating unique, yet suitable, images that go beyond a pictorial representation of traditional family–associate relationships (Anderson, 1999; Murray,

1965). For the purpose of the AAT, the sport corollary is coach–athlete, athlete–athlete, athlete–adversary, and a range of interpersonal relations (father–son, mother–daughter, siblings, peers).

The AAT has already been used with some encouraging results. For example, Thompson and Andersen (2012) reported using AAT images in a case study with a rugby player experiencing adjustment issues and mood disorder. The AAT images were pivotal in developing the relationship between the sport psychologist (i.e., Thompson) and the client. AAT images also opened doors to help the client work through racial and familial power imbalances he had experienced. Thompson and Andersen, however, cautioned that sport psychologists without a deep understanding of psychodynamic methods can underestimate interpretable AAT material. Kavanagh (2010) used six AAT images with the aim of providing an in-depth understanding of the character, motivations, anxiety, and hopes of "Craig," a tennis coach. Despite some initial scepticism about using the AAT images, Kavanagh found they were useful in providing avenues for dialogue not easily approached through standard sport psychology research interviews. Furthermore, Kavanagh reported that although the interpretation process was challenging, her initial doubts about the AAT vanished once she gained experienced administering and using content import techniques to interpret AAT stories. The AAT was particularly beneficial for engaging Craig and allowed him to relax and gave him considerable freedom to engage in dialogue.

In the next section, we offer an example of an athlete's response to two of the AAT images (see Image 3 and Image 6 in Figure 2.1). Accompanying the athlete's tales for these images are two analyses: a mainstream sport psychology thematic interpretation, and a psychodynamic exploration of what the responses might suggest lie beneath the manifest stories.

A thrice told tale: Jenny and Images 3 and 6

Jenny's story Image 3

This image appears to be after a goal has been scored. The central character is finding it hard to believe she has just let the other team score and put them in a position to win. She is blaming herself and has a bad feeling that she has let the team down. The other girls are celebrating and rubbing her mistake in her face. Her coach is in the background, and she is worried about what he is thinking of her and can see his body language; looks as if he is pissed off. I think she will continue to blame herself even if her team-mates and coach don't. Her team will lose because of her mistake.

Sport psychology analysis and interpretation

All interpretations of images are tentative, speculative, and open to modification. On another day, depending on what has happened recently to Jenny, she might tell quite a different story. Jenny's stories and her world cannot, and should not, be finalised in any way. Her responses to the AAT images and their interpretations are hypothetical best guesses, more for starting places to have discussions with Jenny than as sources for any definitive assessment of her.

Jenny identified with the female athlete walking away from the opposition players who are celebrating. Jenny described the central character as despondent and feeling shame or humiliation, especially in relation to the coach in the background. The primary sport psychology theme for Image 3 is competitive anxiety, with secondary themes being social-task cohesion, competitive attributions, and self-efficacy. Jenny's story was primarily focused on sport themes of negative attributional style, negative self-talk, and self-efficacy. An arresting moment in Jenny's story is when she describes the humiliation of the other girls "rubbing her mistake in her face." For Jenny, it appears that she is personally responsible for actions, and mistakes are absolute and final. There is some use of catastrophic descriptions of the sport situation apparent in Jenny's language. Jenny appears to have negative internal attributions (possibly "I'm no good; no one thinks I'm any good"). She cuts a lonely figure, ostracised by her coach, ignored by team-mates, and ridiculed by opponents. Jenny also identified some perceived internal pressures of performing (e.g., letting the other team score, letting the team down, losing because of her mistake). There appears to be little closeness or identification with the team in Jenny's story. Jenny describes herself as being a member of a team, but her story has no descriptions relating to belonging to or the cohesiveness of this team. Jenny did not introduce team-mates into her story as working together to achieve goals and taking responsibility for mistakes as a team. Rather, Jenny described the influence of external demands from the coach and opponents toward the lone figure (central character). Questions may be raised and discussed with Jenny regarding issues such as: others "rubbing her mistake in her face" and letting others down, how she defines "pissed off" in relation to the male coach's feelings toward her, and why others are "annoyed" at her mistakes (especially in a team setting).

Psychodynamic analysis and interpretation

Overall Jenny's story is a tale of the agony of defeat. In response to this image, Jenny appears to self-blame for poor performance. Also, Jenny may have a strongly internalised self-image as a "loser," and her story reveals an isolation and alienation from others. Jenny's anxieties about the father-like coach could reflect unresolved parent–child conflicts, such as parental love being contingent on good performance along with severe negative parental responses (anger) to the child's mistakes. In this image, the coach remains in the background, and the girl is "worried about what he is thinking of her and can see his body language; looks as if he is pissed off." A possible dynamic interpretation of those words "in the background" might reflect that the angry punishing father is metaphorically omnipresent in many other aspects of Jenny's life. In this way, he might also represent the severe internal critic of her superego, a critic so severe that even when others do not blame her, she continues to blame herself. Her last sentence about her mistake causing the team to lose might indicate that Jenny feels responsible for the anger, sadness, or even happiness of others. Children often take on the responsibility for significant others' (e.g., parents, siblings) emotional states. Perceived parental happiness, sadness, or anger get tied to what the child does, or does not do, and when actions or inactions result in negative parental emotions, then the child has failed at making Mum or Dad happy (the child's main job), and shame and humiliation come crashing down. Respondents may not view older male (or female) figures on the AAT images as direct parent representatives, but Jenny's response to this image appears to have strong family dynamics present.

> **Jenny and Image 6**
>
> This is a group of kids, and a couple of them look to be either brother or sister or very close friends. They look like they are about to play soccer. At the moment, it looks like they are having trouble picking the teams. This is because they all don't agree it is fair. The boy with his leg on the ball is the oldest, and he has the responsibility of picking the next player, but he can't decide because the two players left don't look that good. One of the players to choose from is his sister, and he wants to pick her because he doesn't want her to be the last picked, but the problem is that she is shit at soccer. He knows he is the best player and wants to have the best team, but he has to be fair because the others look up to him. I think they won't end up playing as they won't be able to agree on teams. They will just have a kick around and go home for tea.

Sport psychology analysis and interpretation

Jenny described the boy with his foot on the ball as the oldest player who is feeling pressure from others to make a decision on team selection. The primary sport psychology theme for Image 6 is group cohesion, with secondary themes being leadership and team dynamics, confidence, inclusion/exclusion, and rejection. Jenny's story appears to be focused on these sport themes. Jenny indicated that the central character was feeling in a position of responsibility for making a decision that would satisfy all the other children. There was also some conflict for Jenny with the boy's responsibility of picking the next player and feeling that although the girl (the central character's sister) is not good at soccer, there is some pressure to choose her. Questions may be raised and discussed with Jenny regarding issues such as shouldering the responsibility for others' happiness, and why she interprets the central character's decision as important for his and others' enjoyment. Also of potential interest to examine with Jenny would be the conflict of wanting to "have the best team," "being fair," and pressure to choose his (her) sister even though "she is shit at soccer." Jenny's response integrated feelings of inclusion/exclusion, rejection, and a strong relationship with a sibling.

Psychodynamic analysis and interpretation

Jenny's story, at first read, seems to be about the older, dominant boy, but Jenny probably identifies with the sister who is "shit at soccer." Given themes evident in Jenny's responses to the other images, she likely identifies with the incompetent young girl who makes mistakes, who is a loser, but who wants to be chosen and have a go. The older competent boy may represent an actual older sibling, or if Jenny does not have an older sibling, then he may represent a fantasised older brother whom she wanted to have around and admire (like some of her other female friends probably had growing up). I did not have a family history on Jenny, so these thoughts are quite speculative. This story may be about wanting to be "chosen," and that desire holds all sorts of possibilities (to be loved, to be valued). The need to be chosen and valued are thwarted because she is not especially talented at what she wishes to be chosen for. Jenny may feel that worthiness, attention, and love are contingent on playing well, and she knows she does not have the skills that equate to that worthiness. The older, admired (he is the "best" player) brother is a positive authority figure, but he is caught up in the values of sport (he wants the best team) and cannot make a decision between brotherly protection (he does not want her to be the last one chosen) and being the best. I think the central theme of this story is that there is no solution for Jenny. She may see no practical solution to her desire for love and her perceived lack of the qualities (sport skills) that she believes will bring her the desired status of being *chosen* and loved. Jenny may feel stuck with no way out.

The above are brief examples of how someone with a psychodynamic orientation might begin to analyse Jenny's responses. For many in sport psychology, this territory would be rather foreign, and some might even assert that this approach is spinning Freudian fairy tales. We would disagree and suggest that this approach may be helpful if an athlete, such as Jenny, is interested in a deeper exploration of her life, rather than being taught a relaxation or mindful technique to help manage her competition anxiety.

Thoughtful analysis and interpretation of AAT responses may provide an in-depth and idiographic understanding of athletes' characteristics, motivations, and anxieties, as well as assisting in the assessment of personality features. At the very least, discussion of AAT responses can be a useful way of initiating dialogue, engaging the client, and possibly unmasking issues that might otherwise lay dormant (latent personal issues of which athletes may not be consciously aware or reluctant to voice openly). Further, the use of the AAT may help sport psychologists identify and assess personality features relevant to performance and the health and wellbeing of athletes. We recommend that the AAT is not used as a stand-alone instrument, but rather in conjunction with other sources of information (e.g., questionnaires, intake interviews, ongoing service delivery encounters).

Stories from one, two, or three images can be instructive but fall short of a comprehensive tale. Rather, it is when all 10 images, and the stories attached to them, are examined that major themes in athletes' lives are more likely to emerge. With a full 10-image protocol, the amount and depth of information gleaned can be substantial, but the responses to the images are gross symbolic maps of the territories of athletes' heads and hearts, and we must not mistake the maps for the territories. Maps are starting points for discussions with clients about what they might or might not say. In these conversations with athletes we may find that the maps resonate with what athletes feel and think, or we may find that the maps were incomplete, and the tale is more complex and convoluted than we first thought. In any case, the responses to the images are ideal starting places to hold conversations about athletes' worlds, and those conversations can also help consolidate the therapeutic relationship between athlete and sport psychologist.

Future directions and ongoing challenges

In its present state, we believe the AAT contains a substantial variety of apperceptive stimuli that reflect many issues, concerns, and problems athletes experience. There were practicalities to be addressed during the development of the final image set (e.g., sequencing of image presentation, administrative time restraints, choice of interpretation viewpoints), and further research should inform ongoing refinements in procedures and scoring. There are numerous potential uses of the AAT, for example, applied service delivery, multi-method personality research, case-study research, and postgraduate sport psychology training programs. One potential fruitful avenue for research with this technique would be as an adjunct to narrative analysis research to supplement the data gathered in qualitative interviews (see Kavanagh, 2010).

We recommend that practitioners use the entire AAT set of 10 images. Depending on the background, experience, and level of confidence in projective instrument use, sport psychologists have a variety of analysis options available to assist them in interpreting responses of athletes to the AAT images (see Chapter 5). There should, however, be some balance between the accessibility and responsible use of the AAT. One issue with the use of projective methods for sport psychologists is the level of investment practitioners are willing to make. As Bellak (1950) suggested, psychologists should be aware of their own technical and knowledge limitations and take reasonable care when interpreting the results of projective methods. Understanding the theoretical basis of projective techniques requires at least a general understanding of interpretive methods and psychodynamic concepts. Jenkins (2007) stated, "Like the Rorschach, TAT story protocols provide a literal embarrassment of richness that is daunting for students and can be exhausting for experts" (p. 5). Familiarising oneself with the theory, administration, analysis, and interpretation of a projective instrument involves a considerable investment in time, ongoing education, and substantial experience with the instrument.

From the outset, our main objective was developing a new sport projective technique. There are numerous questions and directions that warrant follow-up research with the AAT. Whether the current AAT image set is comprehensive enough for tapping a large range of issues, themes, and complexities that confront athletes is uncertain. We believe further supplementary AAT stimuli could be developed (from some images that we reluctantly culled) to examine specific issues and conflicts or as adjuncts for further exploration of particular themes of interest. Similarly, complementary image sets designed for special populations (e.g., coaches, athletes with disabilities) would likely be of particular benefit for practitioners.

Morgan and Murray's (1935) original intent, in developing the TAT, was not to produce an instrument to test psychodynamic theories of personality, but rather to produce a tool to help clinicians explore the unconscious motivations, dreams, desires, hopes, and fears of their clients. A central by-product of administering the TAT (and the AAT, we hope) and working through the narratives that clients produce is developing a better understanding of clients' internal (and external) worlds. Also, the sharing and exploring of the stories clients produce have the potential to deepen the therapeutic bond and open up further channels for working together. As the stories are discussed and analysed, clients may, in the words of Siegel (2010), "feel felt." That *feeling felt*, understood, and cared for are foundational features for developing therapeutic relationships that heal.

The emerging fields of interpersonal neurobiology (e.g., Cozolino, 2014; Siegel, 2010) and the neuroscience of psychotherapy are confirming many of the core tenets of psychodynamic theory (e.g., unconscious motivation, the importance of early childhood experiences, the healing power of therapeutic relationships). We believe the TAT and the AAT tap into these core features of many helping professions and contribute to the power of the therapeutic relationship to facilitate healing. There is some early and preliminary evidence that the AAT can be a powerful tool in aiding therapists' understandings of their clients and the strengthening of the working alliance. This evidence was demonstrated in the Thompson and Andersen (2012) study of how the AAT, the stories told, and the interpersonal discussions of those narratives helped further understanding and closeness between therapist and client and led to healing. Our ultimate question about the AAT is not a research, or a particularly rigorous scientific, one, but rather a pragmatic and real-world question: Is the AAT useful when carrying out psychological work with athletes and coaches? Our tentative answer is, we believe so.

Conclusion

Murray (1938) insisted that no isolated piece of behaviour could be understood without taking into account the fully functioning person. Murray's crusade has continued through the studies of many researchers over a period of 70 years, and although his *personology* theory has been eclipsed, his projective techniques remain popular with clinicians.

We consider the AAT a *technique* rather than a *test.* For example, Bellak and Abrams (1997) insisted that the Children's Apperception Test (CAT) is not really a test, but a "technique that lends itself to many different uses" (p. 345). According to Rabin (1959), the CAT, like most projective "tests," is a clinical technique rather than a test and, as with other projective techniques, the types of data one obtains using the CAT are not easily translated into numbers. Like the CAT, the AAT is not usually scored in any literal numeric sense, but there are quantitative scoring systems available for storytelling techniques, and an example is introduced in Chapter 5.

The current form of AAT includes: (a) an adult 10-image set, (b) a supplementary set (AAT-S; 5 additional images), and a children's set (AAT-C; 6 images). The AAT images evoke a range of sport-related themes and latent stimulus properties such as relationships with other athletes and coaches, anxiety and arousal issues, concentration, leadership, team cohesion, preparation and routines, flow and optimal performance, confidence, motivation, attributional styles, and self-talk. Between the AAT, the AAT-S, and the AAT-C, many themes can be evoked, and we believe future research will demonstrate the depth and breadth of themes and stories that these images can produce. Moreover, the use of the AAT may help sport psychologists identify and assess personality features relevant to performance and the health and wellbeing of athletes. Sport psychology, as a research and applied discipline, and sport psychologists, in general, have embraced a *Weltanschauung*, where standardised tests, self-reports, and quantitative models, have dominated. We are hopeful that this work will open a dialogue between researchers and practitioners over the potential applications of this projective technique.

Note

1 Most of this chapter was previously published as: Gibbs, P., Marchant, D., & Andersen, M. B. (2016, pre-print online publication). Development of a clinical sport projective assessment method: The Athlete Apperception Technique. *Qualitative Research in Sport, Exercise and Health.* Available from www.tandfonline.com/eprint/zyh2DwhchuK2U9KT9HgT/full

References

American Educational Research Association, A. P. A., and National Council on Measurement in Education. (1999). *The standards for educational and psychological testing* (2nd ed.). Washington, DC: American Educational Research Association.

Andersen, M. B. (Ed.). (2000). *Doing sport psychology*. Champaign, IL: Human Kinetics.

Andersen, M. B. (Ed.). (2005). *Sport psychology in practice*. Champaign, IL: Human Kinetics.

Anderson, J. W. (1999). Henry A. Murray and the creation of the Thematic Apperception Test. In L. Geiser & M. I. Stein (Eds.), *Evocative images: The Thematic Apperception Test and the art of projection* (pp. 23–38). Washington, DC: American Psychological Association.

Anzieu, D. (1960). *Les méthodes projectives*. Paris, France: P.U.F.

Basu, J. (2014). Psychologists' ambivalence toward ambiguity: Relocating the projective test debate for multiple interpretative hypotheses. *Journal of Projective Psychology & Mental Health, 21*, 25–36.

Bellak, L. (1950). The Thematic Apperception Test in clinical use. In L. E. Abt & L. Bellak (Eds.), *Projective psychology* (pp. 185–229). New York, NY: Grove Press.

Bellak, L., & Abrams, D. M. (1997). *The Thematic Apperception Test, the Children's Apperception Test, and the Senior Apperception Technique in clinical use* (6th ed.). Boston, MA: Allyn & Bacon.

Bellak, L., & Bellak, S. S. (1949). *Children's Apperception Test*. Larchmont, NY: C.P.S.

Bellak, L., & Bellak, S. S. (1973). *A manual for the Senior Apperception Technique* (Rev. ed.). Larchmont, NY: C.P.S.

Bouet, M. A. (1970). A projective test for sport participants. In G. S. Kenyon (Ed.), *Contemporary psychology of sport* (pp. 747–752). Chicago, IL: Athletic Institute.

Conroy, D. E., & Benjamin, L. S. (2001). Psychodynamics in sport performance enhancement consultation: Application of an interpersonal theory. *The Sport Psychologist*, *15*, 103–117. doi:10.1123/tsp.15.1.103

Cozolino, L. (2014). *The neuroscience of human relationships: Attachment and the developing social brain* (2nd ed.). New York, NY: Norton.

Crocker, L., & Algina, J. (1986). *Introduction to classical and modern test theory*. New York, NY: Holt, Rinehart, & Winston.

Cronbach, L. J. (1990). *Essentials of psychological testing* (5th ed.). New York, NY: Harper Collins.

Dunn, J. G. H., Bouffard, M., & Rogers, W. T. (1999). Assessing item content-relevance in sport psychology scale-construction research: Issues and recommendations. *Measurement in Physical Education & Exercise Science*, *3*, 15–36. doi:10.1207/s15327841mpee0301_2

Gibbs, P. M. (2006). *Development of the Athlete Apperception Technique (AAT)* (Unpublished doctoral dissertation). Victoria University, Melbourne, VIC, Australia.

Gibbs, P. M. (2010). Psychological assessment: Projective techniques. In S. J. Hanrahan & M. B. Andersen (Eds.), *Routledge handbook of applied sport psychology: A comprehensive guide for students and practitioners* (pp. 101–110). Milton Park, Abingdon, England: Routledge.

Gibbs, P. M., Marchant, D., & Andersen, M. B. (2005). Development of the Athlete Apperception Technique (AAT). In T. Morris, P. Terry, S. Gordon, S. Hanrahan, L. Ievleva, G. Kolt, & P. Tremayne (Eds.), *ISSP 11th world congress of sport psychology: Promoting health and performance for life* (pp. 1–3), [CD-ROM]. Sydney, NSW, Australia: International Society of Sport Psychology.

Giges, B. (2000). Removing psychological barriers: Clearing the way. In M. B. Andersen (Ed.), *Doing sport psychology* (pp. 17–31). Champaign, IL: Human Kinetics.

Haynes, S. N., Richard, D. C. S., & Kubany, E. S. (1995). Content validity in psychological assessment: A functional approach to concepts and methods. *Psychological Assessment*, *7*, 238–247. doi:10.1037/1040–3590.7.3.238

Henry, W. E. (1956). *The analysis of fantasy: The Thematic Apperception Technique in the study of personality*. New York, NY: Wiley.

Hibbard, S. (2003). A critique of Lilienfeld et al.'s (2000) "The scientific status of projective techniques." *Journal of Personality Assessment*, *80*, 260–271. doi:10.1207/S15327752JPA8003_05

Hill, K. L. (2001). *Frameworks for sport psychologists: Enhancing sport performance*. Champaign, IL: Human Kinetics.

Jenkins, S. R. (2007). *A handbook of clinical scoring systems for Thematic Apperceptive Techniques*. Mahwah, NJ: Erlbaum.

Kavanagh, T. E. (2010). *Transitions to the other side of the net: Tales of tennis players who become coaches* (Unpublished doctoral dissertation). Victoria University, Melbourne, VIC, Australia.

Lilienfeld, S. O., Wood, J. M., & Garb, H. N. (2000). The scientific status of projective techniques. *Psychological Science in the Public Interest*, *1*, 27–66. doi:10.1111/1529–1006.002

Lynn, M. R. (1986). Determination and quantification of content validity. *Nursing Research, 35*, 382–385. doi:10.1097/00006199–198611000–00017

Mehrens, W. A., & Lehmann, I. J. (1987). *Using standardized tests in education.* New York, NY: Longman.

Messick, S. (1975). The standard problem: Meaning and values in measurement and evaluation. *American Psychologist, 30*, 955–966. doi:10.1037/0003–066X.30.10.955

Messick, S. (1989). Validity. In R. L. Linn (Ed.), *Educational Measurement* (3rd ed.), pp. 13–103. New York, NY: American Council on Education: Macmillan.

Missoum, G., & Laforestrie, R. (1985). L'image de soi du sportif. *Bulletin de Psychologie, 38*, 909–917.

Morgan, C. D., & Murray, H. A. (1935). A method for investigating fantasies: The Thematic Apperception Test. *Archives of Neurology and Psychiatry, 34*, 289–306. doi:10.1001/archneurpsyc.1935.02250200049005

Morgan, W. G. (2002). Origin and history of the earliest Thematic Apperception Test pictures. *Journal of Personality Assessment, 79*, 422–445. doi:10.1207/S15327752JPA7903_03

Murray, H. A. (1938). *Explorations in personality: A clinical and experimental study of fifty men of college age.* New York, NY: Oxford University Press.

Murray, H. A. (1943). *Thematic Apperception Test manual.* Cambridge, MA: Harvard University Press.

Murray, H. A. (1965). Uses of the Thematic Apperception Test. In B. I. Murstein (Ed.), *Handbook of projective techniques* (pp. 435–442). New York, NY: Basic Books.

Ostrow, A. C. (1998). *Directory of psychological tests in the sport and exercise sciences* (2nd ed.). Morgantown, VA: Fitness Information Technology.

Rabin, A. I. (1959). Children's Apperception Test. In O. Buros (Ed.), *The fifth mental measurements yearbook* (p. 218). Highland Park, NJ: Gryphon Press.

Reber, A. S. (1995). *The Penguin dictionary of psychology* (2nd ed.). New York, NY: Penguin Putnam.

Sherwood, E. T. (1957). On the designing of TAT pictures with special reference to a set for African people assimilating Western culture. *Journal of Social Psychology, 45*, 161–190. doi:10.1080/00224545.1957.9714299

Siegel, D. J. (2010). *The mindful therapist: A clinician's guide to mindsight and neural integration.* New York, NY: Norton.

Teglasi, H. (2001). *Essentials of TAT and other storytelling techniques assessment.* New York, NY: Wiley.

Thompson, C., & Andersen, M. B. (2012). Moving toward Buddhist psychotherapy in sport: A case study. *The Sport Psychologist, 26*, 624–643. doi:10.1123/tsp.26.4.624

Worthen, B. R., Borg, W. R., & White, K. R. (1993). *Measurement and evaluation in the school.* New York, NY: Longman.

3 Properties of the AAT, AAT-S, and AAT-C images

Interpretation and analysis of verbal and written stories have taken many forms since the 1940s. A number of projective test experts (e.g., Bellak, Holt, Lindzey, Murstein, Rabin) have introduced interpretive methods that can be used with both established and recently developed projective techniques. In Chapter 5, we discuss several methods that can be used to interpret and "score" client responses to individual images, as well as themes across an image set. We have included below the basic interpretive method we used to analyse and, ultimately, determine the "best" images for use in the AAT, the AAT-S, and the AAT-C. As previously discussed, we prefer to promote the AAT as an adjunct clinical technique for tapping sport psychology themes and issues rather than a test or inventory.

Below are the sport psychology themes for each image, the *stimulus properties* of the image, and brief gender response variations where applicable. According to Henry (1956), an important part of the interpretation process is to gain a thorough understanding of the stimuli presented to clients. Henry suggested that the interpretation of images requires the examiner to acquire knowledge of several categories of analysis in which the images may be described. The *image properties* for each of the AAT, AAT-S, and AAT-C images are presented below, and each begins by outlining the sport psychology themes "tapped" by images and the latent stimulus demand themes. Described next are the *manifest stimulus demands* (of the images). The manifest aspects are usually observed by respondents and used in their stories (certain aspects of the story that may be considered as given, or represent avoidance, misinterpretation, or distortion) and will also include *adequate stimulus notations* (the major segments of the stimulus respondents frequently use to build a story), *other details often noted* (frequently observed details not referred to in the plot), and *seldom noted details* (details observed or used by a small percentage of respondents). Each image also has a *latent stimulus meaning*; latency is defined as, "existing in hidden form, dormant but capable of being evoked or developed" (Reber, 1995, p. 408). For example, Henry suggested that TAT Card 1 (the picture of a boy with a violin) "is a convenient symbolisation of a person in an ambivalent emotional situation" (p. 48). From an analytic position, the latent stimulus meaning may be the perceived struggle with frustration and authority that is of interest, rather than, for example, attitudes toward the violin (Murstein, 1965). The other criteria outlined for each image, and presented below, are the *form demand, frequent plots, significant variations*, and *gender variations*.

AAT sport psychology themes and stimulus properties

AAT Image 1

Sport psychology themes tapped

competitive anxiety, confidence, fear of failure/success

Latent stimulus demand themes

hierarchal relations, attitudes towards confidence and challenge versus exhaustion and envy, the influence of external demands (expectation, motivation, and relief)

Detailed image stimulus properties

I. *Artist's Description.* Two female athletes compete in the hurdles.
II. *Manifest Stimulus Demand (of the image).* The usual account of this image includes some reference to the two athletes and some explanation of their activity. Other details often noted include some examination of competitive anxiety, self-talk, achievement motivation, confidence, or peer interpersonal relations. Seldom noted details include the hurdles and body language.
III. *Form Demand.* The two figures are the only major details, although the facial features and body language of both athletes can be differently perceived.
IV. *Latent Stimulus Demand.* The basic stimulus is that conveyed by the body language of the athletes and with hierarchal person relations, normally taking the form of the superior (athlete jumping the hurdle) versus the inferior (athlete halting her approach). It is particularly stimulating

of attitudes towards confidence and challenge versus exhaustion and envy, the influence of external demands (expectation, motivation, and relief), and attitudes of personal activity or passivity. This image also frequently integrates ideas of fear of failure or fear or success.

V. *Frequent Plots.* The dominant plot appears to be that of two female athletes in a close and intense battle, and a description of how the race was won. Other plots most frequently take the form of a description of the relationship between the athletes, and respondents tend to focus on the feelings and inner-thoughts or self-talk of the athletes. The athletes are seen as opponents and descriptions of confidence, determination, competition, frustration, mental strength, revenge, persistence, inspiration, and heartbreak are often introduced.

VI. *Significant Variations.* Points of special interest are the extent that extreme reactions of anger and hatred are described.

VII. *Gender Variations.* There are no significant gender response variations.

AAT Image 2 (and AAT-C Image 2C)

Sport psychology themes tapped

achievement motivation, athletic identity, confidence, coach–athlete relationships

Latent stimulus demand themes

hierarchal relations, attitudes toward authority, attitudes toward the influences of external demands, attitudes of personal activity/passivity, father–son relations, attitudes toward rules and regulations

Detailed image stimulus properties

I. *Artist's Description.* A male coach talks to a young male American football player.

II. *Manifest Stimulus Demand (of the image).* The usual account of this image includes only the two males (the person on the right is normally seen as the older or authority figure), and a statement of some relationship between them. Other details often noted include some examination of competitive anxiety, achievement motivation, confidence, and failure.

III. *Form Demand.* The two figures are the only major details.

IV. *Latent Stimulus Demand.* This image deals with hierarchal personal relations, normally taking the form of younger and less experienced versus older and more experienced. Image 2 particularly stimulates attitudes toward authority, toward the influences of external demands, and to a lesser degree, attitudes of personal activity or passivity (especially from the boy's perspective). More specifically, in younger (adolescent or young adult) respondents, the older figure becomes a parent/coach, and stories of a father are stimulated. In older respondents, the older figure (coach) may be interpreted as an impersonal authority figure, and hence, attitudes toward rules and regulations, especially in a professional sport setting, are stimulated.

V. *Frequent Plots.* The plots to this image follow closely the latent stimulus, taking the form most frequently of a father–son or a professional relationship. In any expression, the older is most frequently advising the younger.

VI. *Significant Variations.* Points of special interest deal with the extent that extreme reactions of offence or discord are given versus the usual plots. Also, the characteristics of the relationship stated between the two figures (e.g., goal agreement, authority orientation) are often noted. The outcome is interesting regarding whether the athlete follows the advice mechanically, integrates it into his plans, or rejects it in a hostile manner.

VII. *Gender Variations.* There are two significant gender response variations. First, males are more likely to construct negative outcomes, such as helplessness and disconsolate surrender. Second, males are more likely to focus on the adult figure being a father rather than a coach. To this extent, Image 2 is useful for eliciting feelings towards father–son relations.

AAT Image 3

Sport psychology themes tapped

competitive anxiety, social and task cohesion, competitive attributions, self-efficacy

Latent stimulus demand themes

coach and peer interpersonal relations, feelings towards interpersonal interactions, attitudes toward siblings or parent–child relations

Detailed image stimulus properties

I. *Artist's Description.* A girls' soccer match. In the foreground is a girl walking away from two other girls (opposing players) who are celebrating. In the background, a man (the coach) is looking on.

II. *Manifest Stimulus Demand (of the image).* The usual account of this image includes some reference to the number of persons, to the playing field (specifically soccer), and sometimes accounting for a relationship between the figures. The reference "girls are playing soccer" adequately accounts for the basic stimulus. More frequently, however, the individual figures are identified separately and seen as presented in the artist's description. Frequently noted is some reference to social cohesion, for example, the degree that members of the team respect each other, and some reference to task cohesion, for example, the degree that team members work together to achieve a specific goal. Also frequently referred to is the coach standing in the background, details of the game being played, and the body language of the players.

III. *Form Demand.* The form of this image calls for the respondent to integrate four major form elements, and take into account some aspect of the playing field.

IV. *Latent Stimulus Demand.* This image's basic emotional stimulus is interpersonal relations. The image stimulus deals with the relationship of athletes on opposing teams and in some cases a relationship with a coach. To this extent, it is useful for eliciting feelings towards interpersonal interaction and toward sibling or parent–child relations.

V. *Frequent Plots.* A common plot is the two players celebrating a goal being scored in a soccer match and an opposing player feeling despondent. Also, stories focusing on the despondent player and a mistake she has made are frequently used, as is the perceived disappointment of the coach.

VI. *Significant Variations.* Special points of importance deal with the extent that stimulus details are utilised, the figure chosen as the hero, and the extent that splits occur among the four figures presented. For example, the story may be split so as to unite the two girls celebrating or to unite the despondent girl and the coach, or unite the two girls celebrating and the coach. Similarly, predominance may be given to one figure as the dominant force, with the other figures subordinate. In any of these possible formulations, the attributes of each person and the nature of the interaction between figures are worth special consideration.

VII. *Gender Variations.* There is only one significant gender response variation. Males are more likely than females to identify with the figure in the background (usually referred to as the coach).

AAT Image 4

Sport psychology themes tapped

responses to injury, intrinsic/extrinsic motivation, confidence

Latent stimulus demand themes

despair versus elation, relationship of personal demands to those of outside agents, familiarity of negative emotions, attributional style, passive or assertive nature of personal defences

Detailed image stimulus properties

I. *Artist's Description.* A male athlete laying on a running track.

II. *Manifest Stimulus Demand (of the image).* The usual account of this image includes a reference to the athlete laying on the track and some description of how the athlete progressed to that position. Other details often noted are having collapsed and the issues of coping and responses to injury.

III. *Form Demand.* The form of this image involves the athlete and why he is lying on the track.

IV. *Latent Stimulus Demand.* Image 4 primarily relates to general issues of despair versus elation, and the relationship of personal demands to those of outside agents (e.g., coach, team-mates, crowd). Personal concepts of intrinsic and extrinsic motivation may be revealed.

V. *Frequent Plots.* The basic plots to this image are: (a) runner falls to the ground before the end of the race and is distraught, (b) runner falls to ground after winning the race and is elated, (c) runner falls due to an injury but gets up and courageously finishes the race, (d) runner falls due to an injury and remains on the track in despair.

VI. *Significant Variations.* Any deviation from the preceding may be a significant variation, including any introduced figure, most frequently the coach, the crowd, or a parent, and the attributes of the figure's relationship to any of the above.

VII. *Gender Variations.* One major variation is the manner in which the issue of despair or elation is handled, particularly at the end of the story. Females are more likely to describe a mechanical method to recovery and handling of elation or despair (e.g., catch breath, enjoy the moment) and the outcome (e.g., will get up and try again, will rest before attempting again). Males are more likely to describe an outcome that is grandiose (e.g., wins gold medal, acknowledges the roaring crowd).

AAT Image 5

Sport psychology themes tapped

social-task cohesion, team dynamics, social loafing

Latent stimulus demand themes

interpersonal interactions, the influence of external demands (expectation, motivation, and relief)

Detailed image stimulus properties

I. *Artist's Description.* Three swimmers await the results of competition.

II. *Manifest Stimulus Demand (of the image).* The usual account of this image includes some reference to the number of athletes, and some accounting for the relationship between the figures. Most frequently, the figures' roles are identified as members of a relay team, social cohesion, and some reference to task cohesion (the degree that team members work together to achieve a specific goal). Other details often noted include the importance of the race and the performance of an introduced fourth member of the team. Seldom noted details include the introduction of spectators and opposition swimmers.

III. *Form Demand.* The form of this image calls for the respondent to integrate three major form elements, and to take into account some aspect of the sport situation.

IV. *Latent Stimulus Demand.* This image's basic emotional stimulus resides in the category of interpersonal relations. The image stimulus deals with the relationship of athletes belonging to a relay team. To this extent, it is useful for eliciting feelings towards interpersonal interactions.

V. *Frequent Plots.* The two most frequent plots to this image deal with the issues presented in the discussion of latent stimulus demand. First, the plot of the hero preparing to race and the pressure of either keeping the lead or making up a deficit, or the hero having just completed the race and realising they have lost the lead or made up a deficit. Second, the athletes celebrating a win or feeling despondent in defeat. There may also be stories focusing on an introduced figure who performed poorly and let the team down.

VI. *Significant Variations.* Special points of importance here deal with the extent that stimulus details are used, the figure chosen as the hero figure, and the extent that ruptures occur among the three figures presented. For example, the story may be split so as to bond the two swimmers uniting to blame the other swimmer. Similarly, predominance may be given to any one of the three figures as the leader (dominant) with the other figures subordinate. In any of these possible formulations, the attributes of each person and the nature of the interaction between figures are worth special note.

VII. *Gender Variations.* There are no significant gender response variations.

AAT Image 6 (and AAT-C Image 6C)

Sport psychology themes tapped

group cohesion, leadership and team dynamics, confidence, inclusion/exclusion, rejection

Latent stimulus demand themes

interpersonal relations, relationships of children, inclusion, relationships with siblings, feelings towards interpersonal interactions

Detailed image stimulus properties

I. *Artist's Description.* Six children (three boys and three girls) are organising themselves into teams to play a game.

II. *Manifest Stimulus Demand (of the image).* The usual account of this image includes some reference to the number of persons, to the children already chosen, the physical stance of the remaining characters waiting to be chosen, and some accounting for a relationship between the figures (friends). The reference "kids playing soccer" adequately accounts for the basic stimulus. Individual figures are usually identified separately. Frequently noted is some reference to social cohesion, for example, the degree that members of the team respect each other, and some reference to task cohesion, for example, the degree that team members work together to achieve a specific goal. Seldom noted details include the specifics of the game to be played (soccer, football, etc.), the body language of the children waiting to be picked, and the arrogance or confidence of the boy with his foot on the ball.

III. *Form Demand.* The form of this image calls for the respondent to integrate six major form elements, and to take into account some aspects of the ball.

IV. *Latent Stimulus Demand.* Image 6 is useful for eliciting feelings towards interpersonal interactions and toward sibling relations. Essentially, the image stimulus deals with the relationships of children, inclusion/exclusion, rejection, and, in some cases, relationships with siblings.

V. *Frequent Plots.* The two most frequent plots deal with the issues presented in the discussion of latent stimulus demand. First, the plot of two children waiting to be chosen to join a team. Second, stories focusing on the leaders in the group (specifically the boy with his foot on the ball) and what they are discussing and the decisions being made.

VI. *Significant Variations.* Special points of importance deal with the extent that stimulus details are used, the hero figure chosen, and the extent that ruptures occur among the figures presented. For example, the story may be split to unite two teams of equal number or two groups of children (one with those playing, and one with one or more children excluded). Similarly, predominance may be given to any figure as the dominant force, with the other figures subordinate. In any of these possible formulations, the attributes of each person and the quality of the interactions between the figures are worth special note. Respondents may also introduce physical aggression (fighting, pushing) and verbal abuse (name calling) into their stories.

VII. *Gender Variations.* The only significant variation appears to be the propensity of some males to introduce descriptive taunts (e.g., "four-eyes," "fat kid," "retard").

AAT Image 7

Sport psychology themes tapped

confidence, competitive anxiety

Latent stimulus demand themes

hierarchal personal relations, attitudes toward authority, expectations of others, attitudes of personal activity or passivity, impersonal authority, attitudes toward rules and regulations, mother–daughter relations

Detailed image stimulus properties

I. *Artist's Description.* A woman comforts a girl.

II. *Manifest Stimulus Demand (of the image).* The usual account of this image includes some reference to the two females (the person at the rear normally seen as the older or authority figure) and a statement of some relationship between them. Other details often noted include stories relating to competitive anxiety, achievement motivation, or confidence.

III. *Form Demand.* The two figures are the only major details.

IV. *Latent Stimulus Demand.* This is an image dealing with hierarchal personal relations, normally taking the form of the younger and less experienced versus the older and more experienced. This image is particularly stimulating of attitudes toward authority, toward the influences of external demands (in the person of the older), and to a lesser degree attitudes of personal activity or passivity (especially as seen in the athlete). More specifically in younger (adolescents or young adults) respondents, the older person becomes a parent/coach figure, and images of the mother are stimulated. In older respondents, the older figure/coach may carry the implication of a more impersonal authority and hence attitudes toward rules and regulations, especially in a professional sport setting, are stimulated.

V. *Frequent Plots.* The plots to this image follow closely the latent stimulus, taking the form most frequently of a mother–daughter or a professional relationship. The younger figure is often referred to as the athlete and is usually described as upset or disappointed in the result of a competition. In any formula, the older person is most frequently comforting and advising the younger person.

VI. *Significant Variations.* Points of special interest deal with the extent that extreme reactions of discord are given versus the usual plots. Also, the nature of the relationship between the two figures (e.g., goal agreement, authority orientation) is particularly noted. The outcome becomes most important regarding whether the athlete follows the advice, integrates it into her plans, or rejects the advice with hostility.

VII. *Gender Variations.* There are no significant gender response variations.

AAT Image 8

Sport psychology themes tapped

confidence, competitive anxiety, retirement, achievement motivation

Latent stimulus demand themes

hierarchal personal relations, attitudes toward authority, attitudes toward the influences of external demands, attitudes of personal activity/passivity, impersonal authority, attitudes toward rules and regulations

Detailed image stimulus properties

I. *Artist's Description.* A male baseball player is contemplating his performance. His bag is underneath the bench.
II. *Manifest Stimulus Demand (of the image).* The basic requirements of this image are the athlete and some explanation of the negatively perceived situation. Other details often noted include some examination of competitive anxiety, resilience, vulnerability, achievement motivation, confidence, or retirement. Seldom noted details include some reference to a coach or team-mates and the bag under the bench.
III. *Form Demand.* The single figure is the only basic form.
IV. *Latent Stimulus Demand.* The emotional demand of image 8 is its negative dramatic quality. The stimulus equates to the question: why would a person be depressed or in pain and what would he do about it? In responding to this stimulus, the familiarity of the respondent with negative emotions, optimism or pessimism, and the passive or assertive quality of personal defences are revealed.
V. *Frequent Plots.* The young man is generally seen at some point in an unhappy chain of events (e.g., a bad performance, argument with team-mates or coach). He is often described as upset with his performance, in pain, or disappointed after being sent from the field of play. Themes of guilt and despair are often described.
VI. *Significant Variations.* Any happy and constructive story would seem to be a misperception of this negative image unless the respondent can logically account for the downcast head and the slumped body. Points of interest will be the outcome regarding whether the athlete overcomes his difficulty, the use of any introduced figures (e.g., parent, team-mate, coach), and the roles they play in either creating or resolving the trouble and the previous event to which the difficulty is attributed.
VII. *Gender Variations.* Females are more likely than males to construct a story that begins with a positive/neutral emotional tone (e.g., a moment of solitude before participation, relaxing before the competition). Male responses usually describe a negative introduction to the story (e.g., totally despondent, a failure, hangs his head in sorrow).

AAT Image 9

Sport psychology themes tapped

social and task cohesion, leadership, hierarchal relations

Latent stimulus demand themes

peer interpersonal relations, feelings towards interpersonal interaction, hierarchal person relations, apprehension over body contact, lesbian issues

Detailed image stimulus properties

I. *Artist's Description.* Two female softball players walk off the field in discussion.

II. *Manifest Stimulus Demand (of the image).* The usual account of this image includes some reference to the two athletes and some explanation of their activity. Often explained is the relationship between the women. Also frequently noted is some reference to social cohesion, for example, the degree that members of the team respect each other, and some reference to task cohesion such as the degree that team members work together to achieve a specific goal.

III. *Form Demand.* The two figures are the only major details.

IV. *Latent Stimulus Demand.* The basic emotional stimulus relates to interpersonal relations. The image stimulus deals with the relationship of athletes belonging to a team and usually a discussion of tactics, a reflection, or a mistake. Image 9 may also be used to deal with hierarchal person relations, normally taking the form of the superior (coach, athlete on the left) versus the inferior (player, athlete on the right). The close physical proximity of the bodies readily stimulates apprehension over body contact and sometimes stimulates lesbian themes. Closely related is the possibility of interpreting the scene as peers, buddies, and female companions.

V. *Frequent Plots.* The basic plots follow closely the latent stimulus, taking the form most frequently of a professional relationship. In any formula, the superior (athlete on the left) is most frequently advising the inferior (athlete on the right). The athletes are seen as coach/athlete discussing tactics or building a relationship. Often the coach is seen as advising the athlete or taking her out of the game (as a softball pitcher).

VI. *Significant Variations.* The nature of the relationship stated between the athletes (joint goals, how authority oriented) may be particularly noted. The outcome becomes important regarding how the athletes develop their plans for success.
VII. *Gender Variations.* There are no significant gender response variations.

AAT Image 10

Sport psychology themes tapped

intrinsic/extrinsic motivation, fear of failure/success, attributional style

Latent stimulus demand themes

attitudes towards latent competitive inadequacies, personal attitudes (e.g., arrogance, self-importance, superiority)

Detailed image stimulus properties

I. *Artist's Description.* Four male track athletes cross the finishing line.
II. *Manifest Stimulus Demand (of the image).* The usual account of this image includes some identification of the men as athletes or runners. Other details often noted include a discussion of the relationship between the athletes, attributions (why the race was won or lost), intrinsic/extrinsic motivation, the win/loss outcome, or some reference to personal attitudes (e.g., arrogance, self-importance, superiority).
III. *Form Demand.* This image presents many possibilities of form notation (the clothing, positions, body parts), but the usual forms are the four men.
IV. *Latent Stimulus Demand.* The basic stimulus is that conveyed by the body language of the four runners, and a fear of failure or fear of success. Some respondents describe their latent athletic inadequacies through reactions of the other runners to the man with arms raised.
V. *Frequent Plots.* The dominant plot is a group of male athletes and some description of the outcome and how the race was won. The introduction of dishonour is often discussed with respect to the aftermath of the race (e.g., the winner is found guilty of a banned substance, disqualified, and stripped of medals). Sometime the man with arms raised is described as having celebrated too early, and disqualification or suspension follows.
VI. *Significant Variations.* Respondents often single out individuals of special interest, especially the athlete with arms raised triumphantly.

The winner of the race may be described as "cocky" or "arrogant," and other characters described of "envious" and "hateful."

VII. *Gender Variations.* Female respondents are more likely to describe the winner of the race as gracious. They may also describe the athlete acknowledging others (e.g., competitors, team-mates, coach, family) who have assisted him in his win.

AAT-S (supplementary images) sport psychology themes and stimulus properties

AAT-S Image 1S

Sport psychology themes tapped

competitive anxiety, confidence, vulnerability

Latent stimulus demand themes

peer interpersonal relations, dependency and passivity towards superior uncontrollable force, attitude towards a controlling force, apprehension over body contact, gay male issues

Detailed image stimulus properties

I. *Artist's Description.* Two males prepare for a wrestling bout.

II. *Manifest Stimulus Demand (of the image).* The usual account of this image includes only the two figures and some explanation of the wrestling stance. Generally, the interpretation is consistent with the artist's description and some description of the verbal (or non-verbal) interaction of the characters. Also, frequently noted is some examination of competitive anxiety, vulnerability, or confidence.

III. *Form Demand.* The two figures are the only major details, though the facial features and hand positioning of both athletes can be differently perceived.

IV. *Latent Stimulus Demand.* Responses to Image 1S may reflect the respondent's passivity and attitude towards a controlling force. The close physical proximity of the bodies readily stimulates apprehension over body contact and, sometimes gay male themes. Similarly, the possibility of interpreting the scene regarding peers, buddies, and male companions may reflect the respondent's ease with same-sex interpersonal relations.

V. *Frequent Plots.* There is usually some explanation for the action (e.g., tactic) of the central character. There may also be some explanation of whether the central character is fearful or anxious and is being attacked or restrained. The manner that the issue of despair or elation is handled is often discussed detailing physical or mental tactics (e.g., stamina, motivation, determination).

VI. *Significant Variations.* The reaction to the potentially passive dependent status is of interest.

VII. *Gender Variations.* There are no significant gender response variations.

AAT-S Image 2S

Sport psychology themes tapped

social-task cohesion, intrinsic/extrinsic motivation

Latent stimulus demand themes

interpersonal relations, faith, attitudes toward authority, attitudes toward the influences of external demands, attitudes of personal activity/passivity, impersonal authority

Detailed image stimulus properties

I. *Artist's Description.* A male coach stands above a group of kneeling football players.

II. *Manifest Stimulus Demand (of the image).* The usual account of this image includes some reference to the number of persons, and some accounting for a relationship between the figures, most often a team and a coach. The reference "a team in prayer or thought," however, also may account for the basic stimulus. Frequently noted is some reference to social cohesion (e.g., the degree that members of the team respect each other, team spirit), and some reference to task cohesion (e.g., the degree that team members work together to achieve a specific goal). The body language of the players and the identification of the primary figure as a priest are also sometimes noted.

III. *Form Demand.* The form of this image calls for the respondent to integrate two major form elements: the coach/priest and the playing group/team.

IV. *Latent Stimulus Demand.* This image elicits attitudes toward authority, the influences of external demands, and attitudes of personal activity or passivity (especially as seen in the athletes). More specifically in younger (adolescent or young adult) respondents, the standing figure is generally seen as a parent. In older respondents, the standing figure may carry the implication of a more impersonal authority, and attitudes toward rules and regulations, especially in a professional sport setting, are stimulated.

V. *Frequent Plots.* There are two frequent plots to Image 2S. First, the coach is giving his team an inspirational or motivational speech, and the team is feeling empowered as a group to stand united in success or defeat. Second, the story portrays a focus on a tragedy (e.g., death of a team-mate) and the team supporting each other and uniting with the help of a priest or coach. The outcome of the story may be described as positive or negative.

VI. *Significant Variations.* Points of special interest deal with the introduction of spiritual or religious beliefs to the extent that extreme reactions are given versus the usual plots.

VII. *Gender Variations.* There are no significant gender response variations.

AAT-S Image 3S

Sport psychology themes tapped

achievement motivation, intrinsic/extrinsic motivation, confidence

Latent stimulus demand themes

hierarchal person relations, attitudes towards confidence and challenge versus exhaustion and envy, influence of external demands (expectation, motivation, and relief), attitudes of personal activity/passivity, jealously, gloating, and boasting

Detailed image stimulus properties

I. *Artist's Description.* A female athlete celebrates in front of another athlete sitting on the ground.

II. *Manifest Stimulus Demand (of the image).* The usual account of this image includes only the two figures and a statement of some relationship between them.

III. *Form Demand.* The two figures are the only major details, though the body language of both athletes can be differently perceived. Other details often noted are some discussion of response to injury or over-training, identification of intrinsic or extrinsic motivation, and confidence in sport.

IV. *Latent Stimulus Demand.* This image generally appears to be dealing with hierarchal personal relations, normally taking the form of the superior (athlete with raised arms, "winner") versus the inferior (athlete sitting, "loser"). Image 3S is particularly stimulating of attitudes relating to confidence, challenge versus exhaustion, the influence of external demands (expectation, motivation), and attitudes of personal activity or passivity. This image is also frequently interpreted regressively and feelings of jealously, envy, gloating, and boasting are revealed. The athletes are sometimes described as friends.

V. *Frequent Plots.* The basic plots to the story follow closely the latent stimulus, taking the form most frequently of a professional relationship. In any formula, the standing figure (superior) is most frequently advising the seated figure (inferior). Sometimes the figure on the ground is seen as the hero (already finished the race and relaxing or dealing with an injury) and is providing support and encouragement to the other. The athletes may also be seen as team-mates rather than opponents.

VI. *Significant Variations.* Points of special interest are the extent that extreme reactions of anger and hatred are elicited. The function of the relationship between the athletes is particularly noted (e.g., goal agreement, authority oriented). The outcome becomes important in terms of whether the loser integrates the actions of the winner into their own plans for success or motivation or rejects the actions with hostility.

VII. *Gender Variations.* There are no significant gender response variations.

AAT-S Image 4S

Sport psychology themes tapped

conflict, arousal, authority consequences

Latent stimulus demand themes

peer interpersonal relations, attempt to deny and cover up aggression recognition (or rationalise), familiarity with the passive-assertive nature of personal defences, apprehension over body contact

Detailed image stimulus properties

I. *Artist's Description.* The male athletes confront each other aggressively.
II. *Manifest Stimulus Demand (of the image).* The usual account of this image includes some reference to the two figures and some explanation of their position. Other details often noted are descriptions of increased levels of arousal resulting in strong emotions such as joy, exhilaration, anger, or rage. Seldom noted details include a description of the consequences of their action (e.g., a governing body will enforce some punishment).
III. *Form Demand.* The two figures are the only major details, though the facial features and hand positioning of both athletes can be differently perceived.
IV. *Latent Stimulus Demand.* This image is essentially an aggressive stimulus, and it is interesting to observe how respondents attempt to deny or rationalise aggression in their stories. The stimulus is essentially the question: why would adults (or professional athletes) act in such a manner? In responding to this stimulus, the familiarity of the respondent with the passive or assertive nature of personal defences is often revealed. The close physical proximity of the bodies readily stimulates apprehension over body contact and, sometimes, gay male themes. Similarly, the possibility of interpreting the scene in terms of peers, buddies, and male companions may reflect the respondent's ease with interpersonal same-sex relations. Sometimes a question is raised: "Are they fighting or about to kiss?"
V. *Frequent Plots.* The two basic plots for this image are opponents having an argument or fight, or team-mates celebrating a score or win, or team-mates preparing for the competition or attributing a mistake or loss to each other. The players are generally seen at some point in a chain of events (e.g., a bad or good performance, argument with opposition or officials). The outcome is of special interest in regard to the resolution of the conflict, or a reaction to the event by officials or a governing body.
VI. *Significant Variations.* The success and ease that the respondent provides a "non-aggressive" plot is of special interest. Points of interest here will be the outcome in terms of the use of any introduced figures (e.g., opposition player, team-mate, coach) and the roles they play in either creating or diffusing the situation.
VII. *Gender Variations.* Male responses are more likely to describe the situation as team-mates celebrating and "firing each other up," and are more likely to report a positive outcome (e.g., win the game and celebrate, mates banding together).

AAT-S Image 5S (and AAT-C Image 3C)

Sport psychology themes tapped

achievement motivation, confidence

Latent stimulus demand themes

hierarchal personal relations, attitudes toward authority and influences of external demands, attitudes of personal activity/passivity, impersonal authority, attitudes toward rules and regulations

Detailed image stimulus properties

I. *Artist's Description.* A male coach assists a female athlete with a pole vault training session.

II. *Manifest Stimulus Demand (of the image).* The usual account of this image includes some reference to the two figures (the person on the right normally seen as the older or authority figure), and a statement of some relationship between them. Other details often included are explanations of the relationship between the figures, identification of intrinsic or extrinsic motivation, and confidence in sport.

III. *Form Demand.* There are only two details, the man and the athlete, that require attention.

IV. *Latent Stimulus Demand.* This image relates to hierarchal personal relations, normally taking the form of the younger and less experienced (athlete) along with an older and more experienced (coach). Image 5S is particularly stimulating of attitudes toward authority and influences of external demands in the person of the older, and to a lesser degree, attitudes of personal activity or passivity, especially as seen in the athlete. More specifically, in younger respondents, adolescent or young adult, the older person becomes a parent/coach figure, and images of the father are stimulated. In older respondents, the older figure/coach may evoke impersonal authority and attitudes toward rules and regulations, especially in a professional sport setting.

V. *Frequent Plots.* The plots follow closely the latent stimulus, taking the form most frequently of a father–daughter or a professional relationship. In any formula, the older is most frequently advising the younger in regards to learning or perfecting a skill.

VI. *Significant Variations.* Points of special interest deal with the characteristics of the relationship stated between the two figures (e.g., goal agreement, authority orientation). Sometimes the authority figure is described as pressuring (literally pushing) the athlete to succeed as representative of their own desires (father–daughter). The outcome becomes most important in terms of whether the athlete follows the advice, integrates it into her own plans, or rejects it with hostility.

VII. *Gender Variations.* There are no significant gender response variations.

AAT-C (children's images) sport psychology themes and stimulus properties

AAT-C Image 1C

Sport psychology themes tapped

confidence, achievement motivation, vulnerability, competitive anxiety

Latent stimulus demand themes

attitudes toward authority and influences of authority demands, attitudes of personal activity/passivity, attitudes toward rules and regulations, identification with the athletic role

Detailed image stimulus properties

I. *Artist's Description.* A young male baseball player sits next to players standing.

II. *Manifest Stimulus Demand (of the image).* The basic requirements of this image are only the young male and some explanation of the perceived situation. Other details often noted include some examination of competitive anxiety, achievement motivation, or confidence.

III. *Form Demand.* The form of this image calls for the respondent to integrate two major elements (the boy and the "others"), and to take into account some aspect of the sport situation.

IV. *Latent Stimulus Demand.* This image particularly stimulates attitudes toward authority, toward the influences of authority demands (e.g., parent, coach), and to a lesser degree, attitudes of personal activity or passivity from the boy's perspective. More specifically, attitudes toward rules and regulations, especially in a professional sport setting, are stimulated. The boy is also often seen as struggling with the degree that he identifies with the athletic role.

V. *Frequent Plots.* Constructed plots to Image 1C usually take the form of a boy waiting for his turn to perform. The hero is often described as disgruntled, annoyed, disappointed, lonely, stubborn, and lacking confidence. The two most frequent plots to this image deal with the issues presented in the discussion of latent stimulus demand. First, there is the plot of a coach or parent refusing to let the boy play, due mainly to a poor attitude, lack of skill, or simply waiting his turn. Second, stories portraying a focus on being ignored entirely by authority figures. The outcome of the story may be described as positive or negative.

VI. *Significant Variations.* Points of special interest deal with the extent that extreme reactions of offence or discord are given versus the usual plots. Also the nature of the relationship stated between the hero and introduced figures (e.g., coach, parents, siblings) be particularly noted. The outcome becomes important in terms of whether the boy becomes annoyed with authority figures, blames them for his position on the bench, sulks and blames others, or overcomes and continues with his sport.

VII. *Gender Variations.* There are no significant gender response variations.

AAT-C Image 2C (see AAT Image 2 above)

AAT-C Image 3C (see AAT-S Image 5S above)

AAT-C Image 4C

Sport psychology themes tapped

confidence, social facilitation/debilitation, injury response

Latent stimulus demand themes

negative dramatic quality, success/failure, attributional style, passive/assertive nature of personal defences

Detailed image stimulus properties

I. *Artist's Description.* A baseball player sits on the baseball field with a crowd cheering/jeering in background.

II. *Manifest Stimulus Demand (of the image).* The basic requirements of this image are only the player (male or female) and some explanation of the seated position and generally negatively perceived situation. Some description of the crowd in the background, the player's equipment, and the "base" (softball/baseball) is also sometimes noted.

III. *Form Demand.* The single figure and the background crowd are the only basic forms.

IV. *Latent Stimulus Demand.* The emotional demand of this image is the negative dramatic quality and the beliefs that athletes possess regarding their abilities to succeed in their chosen sports. In responding to this stimulus the familiarity of the respondent with negative emotions, optimism or pessimism, and the passive or assertive nature of personal defences are revealed.

V. *Frequent Plots.* Generally, the player is seen at some point in an unhappy chain of events (e.g., a poor performance, argument with team-mates or coach). The player may be upset, crying, or in pain. Ideas of guilt, despair, and hopelessness are often described, sometimes resulting from taunts of the crowd.

VI. *Significant Variations.* Often any happy and constructive story is a misperception of this negative image, unless the respondent can logically account for the downcast head and slumped body. Points of interest are the outcome in terms of whether or not the player overcomes the difficulty, the use of any introduced figures (e.g., team-mate, coach, relative, friend) and their roles in either having created the trouble or in getting the player out of it, and the previous event to which the difficulty is attributed. The introduction of serious injuries and need for medical attention are also significant variations.

VII. *Gender Variations.* The main gender variation appears to be a generally positive outcome in female stories (e.g., determination to play better next match/season) and generally negative outcomes in males (e.g., will never recover, retire, attacked by the crowd). Males are also more likely to focus on injuries and medical attention.

AAT-C Image 5C

Sport psychology themes tapped

self-talk, confidence, parent–coach (father–son) interpersonal relations

Latent stimulus demand themes

attitudes toward authority, attitudes toward the influences of external demands, attitudes of personal activity/passivity

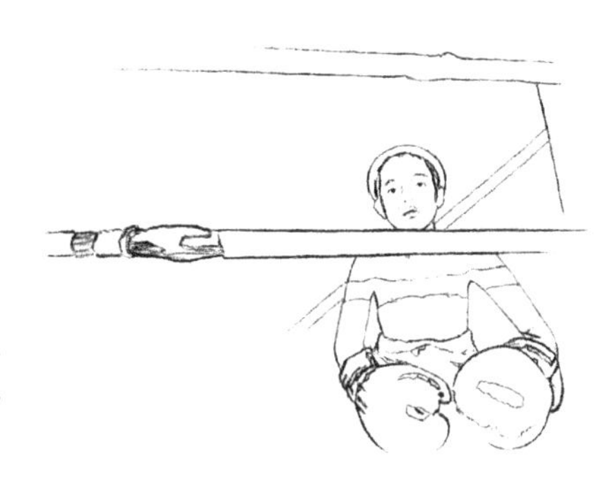

Detailed image stimulus properties

I. *Artist's Description.* A boy looks out from a boxing ring.
II. *Manifest Stimulus Demand (of the image).* The basic requirements of this image are only the young male and some explanation of why he is in a boxing ring. Other details often noted include some examination of the belief or degree of certainty the boy possesses about his ability, and the belief that his behaviour will lead to success.
III. *Form Demand.* The form of this image is simple involving the major stimulus elements: the boy and the boxing ring.
IV. *Latent Stimulus Demand.* Image 5C is particularly stimulating of attitudes toward authority, toward the influences of external demands (in the person of introduced father figures), and to a lesser degree, attitudes of personal activity or passivity (especially as seen in the boy). More specifically introduced figures are usually parents or a coach and particularly images of the father are stimulated.
V. *Frequent Plots.* Normally the figure is the hero in the general sense, and the sympathy of the storyteller is with him. That is, the boy is feeling disappointed, embarrassed, disoriented, or feeling that his ego, confidence, or self-esteem is crushed. Stories also generally introduce feelings of inferiority and lack of skill or physical prowess. The boy is often described as dreaming about being as good as his father someday, feeling anxious and insecure, being inspired by others, attentive and unafraid, or fearless.
VI. *Significant Variations.* It is useful to note stories about the outcome of the fight in respect to injuries and medical attention. The respondent's desire for recognition and their fears of vulnerability may also be noted.
VII. *Gender Variations.* There are no significant gender response variations.

AAT-C Image 6C (see AAT Image 6 above)

References

Henry, W. E. (1956). *The analysis of fantasy: The Thematic Apperception Techniques in the study of personality.* New York, NY: Wiley.

Murstein, B. I. (1965). The stimulus. In B. I. Murstein (Ed.), *Handbook of projective techniques* (pp. 509–546). New York, NY: Basic Books.

Reber, A. S. (1995). *The Penguin dictionary of psychology* (2nd ed.). New York, NY: Penguin Putnam.

4 Administration procedures for the AAT, AAT-S, and AAT-C

In this chapter, we describe the instructions for clients and the various administration formats for the AAT including individual (one-on-one) testing, group administration, and a take-home version. This chapter includes a response booklet, instructions, and image worksheets (presented below). For a group administration and a "take-home" completion of the AAT, photocopy from this manual and print (or download from the e-version), along with images from Chapter 6.

As the test developers, we encourage interested sport and clinical psychology researchers and practitioners to use the AAT in practice and scientific investigations. To this end, we have produced this test manual to guide future research and applied use of the AAT. As Bellak (1950) suggested, however, even the most experienced practitioners should take reasonable care when administering projective techniques (instruments) and interpreting the results. Understanding the theoretical basis, administration guidelines, and considerations, and scoring procedures of projective techniques requires at least a general understanding of interpretive methods and psychodynamic concepts, but clinical and sport psychologists need not have extensive training in psychodynamic theory to pull major themes from athletes' responses to images. Nevertheless, some knowledge of manifest and latent content would be helpful. The information that is generated from the AAT may overlap with information garnered from observations, interviews, and other testing. The AAT represents an alternative, or adjunct, tool to many of the quantitative tests currently used by sport psychologists, and in this chapter (and in Chapter 5), we will outline some basic guidelines for the administration and the scoring/interpretation/analysis of the AAT, along with some of the theoretical foundations and practical considerations underpinning such guidelines.

Projective technique attributes in administration

Rabin (1968) labelled two general attributes that identify projective techniques *primary* and *secondary*. The primary attribute incorporates the most distinctive feature of projective techniques (e.g., sensitivity to unconscious or latent aspects of personality). The secondary attribute incorporates the ambiguity of the stimulus presented to the person. The ambiguity of the stimulus is the most frequently proposed quality for distinguishing projective techniques from other types of tests. The first consideration of the primary attribute is that projective techniques are often presumed to provide efficient means of tapping into internal characteristics that people find difficult to accept, be aware of, or access. Rabin suggested that projective techniques have the capacity to stimulate private, covert, latent, and unconscious components of individual personalities. It is this capacity that distinguishes projective techniques from most other psychological instruments. There is a matter of conjecture regarding this characteristic of projective techniques. It is not the projective technique itself that adheres to these characteristics; rather, it is a functional outcome of the techniques in the application. In other words, projective techniques provide the means to stimulate unconscious components of personality (the intuitive clinician then uses the data derived from the technique in [one hopes] an effective manner). Another distinctive feature of the primary attribute, according to Rabin, is the *multidimensionality* of projective techniques. Projective techniques are employed for many diverse purposes. Rabin suggested it is hard to conceive of any psychological variable that has not been assessed using a projective method. The next feature of the primary attribute is one that distinguishes projective techniques from other psychological instruments: *limited client/participant understanding of the purpose of the test.* When ordinarily employed, there is usually no full understanding by the person of what the examiner is trying to assess. Often the client or research participant has some general understanding of the goal of the investigator/practitioner, such as the measurement of personality, but the participant or client is usually unaware of what psychological variable the clinician or researchers is exploring. Another facet of the primary attribute is the *multiplicity of responses* that can be elicited because of the ambiguity of the stimuli. Quantitative questionnaires or inventories do not allow people to select responses from a theoretically unlimited number of response alternatives. Using story construction and completion techniques, common to many projective techniques, people are bound only by the restrictions of their language and psychological make-ups. The final feature of the primary attribute is the *profusion and richness of the response data they elicit.* This aspect is intimately connected to the previous one. According to Rabin, projective technique responses far exceed, in sheer quantity, the typical product of an inventory or rating scale. Projective technique response data are usually numerous and also tend to be quite varied. In other words, both the quantity and complexity of responses distinguish projective techniques from conventional personality instruments.

The *secondary* attribute that Rabin (1968) introduced includes distinguishing qualities such as the ambiguity of the stimulus, the appropriateness for holistic analysis, and the tendency to evoke fantasy responses. Projective techniques usually include more ambiguous stimuli than most other psychological instruments. Rabin suggested, however, that stimuli that are meaningful and easy to identify (such as photographs or drawings) can still evoke the same identification as the most ambiguous stimuli. Sometimes, an inkblot can be identified simply as an inkblot. It is only when the person is asked to explain what the inkblot could represent that the stimulus becomes ambiguous. Another characteristic of the secondary attribute is the appropriateness for *holistic analysis* (sensitivity to the *total person*). A holistic analysis of a person points to the necessity of considering patterns and profiles rather than individual scores. The attributes of projective techniques lend themselves to holistic analysis more so than tests with scaling, quantitative structures. A third characteristic of the secondary attribute is the tendency to evoke *fantasy responses*. According to Rabin, even though people may be aware that their responses are linked to realistic situations, they are encouraged to respond imaginatively. Normally, people are instructed that there are no right or wrong responses to the images shown, and they should respond in whatever manner seems most natural and interesting to them.

Individual (one-on-one) administration of the AAT and the AAT-S

Many projective instrument manuals state specific guidelines for the administration of images. In the original TAT manual, Murray suggested that practitioners use a subset of 20 images from the total of 31 images. More specifically, Murray recommended a set of 20 images for males, 20 images for females, and two sub-sets for boys and girls. The majority of TAT-like test authors (e.g., Henry, Eron, Murstien, Murray) recommend using the prescribed TAT image set to gain maximum benefit. Practitioners, however, often have personal preferences for particular images. For example, Bellak (1950) suggested that experienced practitioners often want to gain specific insights into certain areas (e.g., interpersonal relations, parental issues, sexuality concerns) and choose particular images. Similarly, practitioners using the AAT may choose selected images based on a number of constraints or requirements (e.g., time factors, personal interests, preferences, presenting issues, gender-specific issues). We recommend, however, that practitioners use the entire AAT set (10 images). Practitioners may also choose any, or all, of the supplementary images (AAT-S; 5 images) that evoke additional material on specific themes such as apprehension over body contact, vulnerability, arousal/aggression, faith, boasting/gloating, and conflict. The administration guidelines for the AAT-C are discussed below, and the general issues and problems of child/adolescent testing must be taken into account.

Many projective techniques are often administered in a single session, in a particular sequence, over in a reasonably short period (e.g., 30 to 60 minutes). Many projective technique experts (e.g., Murray, Eron, Rabin, Murstein) recommended that image sets be administered over two sessions at least 5 days apart. The majority of projective techniques take 20 to 40 minutes to administer; scoring usually takes approximately 30 minutes, and additional time is required for interpretation. According to Aronow (1995), the major problem with the use of projective techniques is the time-intensive nature of such assessments (one possible reason why projective techniques have not been adopted in sport psychology). We have been mindful of these issues during the planning and development of the AAT, and our applications and use of the AAT indicate that the final image set (10 images) can be administered in a single session (approximately 1 hour). Furthermore, a range of scoring and interpretive options are available to support interpretation (e.g., sport psychology theme analysis; see Chapter 5).

The single most important consideration in AAT administration is providing an atmosphere where the person feels relaxed and comfortable enough to respond spontaneously. The administration should be in a well lit, comfortable, and quiet room so that the client can be free of distractions and interruptions. Following standard thematic apperception technique instructions (e.g., who is the central character, what is happening, what went on before, what will the outcome be), the examiner hands selected images to the client. The instructions to clients that we have used and now recommend, based on Murray's (1943) instructions, are the following:

> I am going to show you some drawings, one at a time, and your job is to make up a story about what is happening. Use your imagination. Tell me what has led up to the event shown in the drawing, describe what is happening at this moment, what the characters are thinking and feeling, and then tell me the outcome and what will happen after this moment. Say what you think as it comes to your mind. There are no right or wrong answers. Do you have any questions? Here is the first drawing.

The instructions can be repeated upon request, and parts of the instructions may have to be repeated later on when reminding the client to elaborate on the central character's thoughts and feelings, or creating a conclusion to the story. The instructions are simplified slightly for children and adults with limited education (Aronow, Weiss, & Reznikoff, 2001).

During administration, Ryan (1985) suggested the examiner, if possible, should not interfere with the client's responses. At times, however, clients should be reminded about parts of the tasks being omitted (e.g., who is the central character, what happened before and after this moment). If the client asks for more detailed instructions or seeks feedback or input from the examiner, examiners should respond openly but noncommittally, such as stating "You may make the story about anything you please." Occasionally some clients, particularly children, may require encouragement, but this should be applied judiciously (Ryan, 1985).

In traditional thematic apperception technique administration, the examiner records the time between presentation of an image and the response. Comments, exclamations, or halting verbalisations given by the client may not be the beginning of the story, although Ryan (1985) suggested they should be noted. The measure of time from image presentation to response is termed the *response latency* and is useful in gauging the client's handling of the specific image. For example, very long response latencies may reflect a struggle or conflict with the material in the image. Conversely, extremely short responses may suggest an impulsive or perhaps counter-phobic approach to the image material. The examiner should record all of the client's verbalisations, including spontaneous verbalisations, extra-test comments, utterings, laughter, and the story response. Also, it is useful to note specific behavioural and affective reactions (e.g., fidgeting, facial expressions, sighs, gestures) that reflect aspects of the client's psychological response. Even though one needs to be aware of and to record all of the above response specifics, the administration of the AAT (and AAT-S and AAT-C) is still relatively simple. The examiner only requires a set of AAT images (and maybe AAT-S images) and, if desired, a recording device, and for recording notes and time, a pad of paper, a pen, and a clock.

Following the administration of the images, examiners may like to obtain further information from the client about specific responses: a procedure termed *the inquiry*. Typically, such inquiries are about clients' possible sources for themes introduced in the storytelling procedure, associations to the images or stories, or emotional reactions to particular stimuli. Examiners can ask clients to recall their most and least favourite images or stories, particularly when a day or more has passed since the actual administration. Finally, the inquiry may be useful in *testing the limits* of certain responses. Examiners can also inquire about aspects of the images that may have been conspicuously omitted or distorted in the stories, or encourage elaborations on themes or stories that were particularly barren or sparse (Ryan, 1985).

Group and take-home administration of the AAT and the AAT-S

The administration guidelines for groups or individual take-home follow much of what is presented above, but with a few minor exceptions. The worksheets for both group and take-home administrations are included below and practitioners/researchers can simply photocopy the relevant pages (or download from the e-version; or make your own up; easy to do by following the template below) and attaching the image set (AAT, AAT-S, AAT-C) required (photocopied from Chapter 6). For the group administration, the examiner may add a time limit if desired, and could read the above instructions verbatim to the group or *ad-lib* the following basics: interpret the scene depicted in the image, identify the central character, explain what is taking place, describe the thoughts and feelings of the characters, describe the preceding events, and speculate on a likely outcome. Participants should be provided a response booklet, instructions, and image worksheets (provided below). Images can be given to participants as a complete image set or projected onto a screen for 5 to 10 minutes each in group presentations. Clients who take the technique home should be given a package to complete and return by a due date (to be determined by the examiner). Included in the package should be the response booklet and instructions (provided below), the number labelled image set(s), the image worksheets (provided below), and possibly a return stamped envelope.

Administration of the AAT-C

In the administration of the AAT-C, general issues and problems of child/adolescent testing must be taken into account. The AAT-C is especially suited to for use with older children and adolescents, but not young children. The administration guidelines for the AAT-C requires the practitioner to be well versed in the administration of tests in general to adolescents and children; however, the AAT-C administration instructions are essentially the same as for the AAT and AAT-S. Bellak and Siegel (1989), the authors of the Children's Apperception Test (CAT), and Bellak and Abrams (1997) recommended that the image set administration for children (and adolescents/children with limited education or intellectual difficulties) be presented more as a game than a test. To build rapport and help the young client to feel at ease, the examiner can explain that it is not a test, and there will be no disapproval, competition, disciplinary action, and so forth. Bellak and Abrams (1997) also suggest that when working with younger clients, it is advisable to keep the full set of images out of sight because children have a tendency to want to play with all the images at once. The AAT-C set includes six images. As children can have a limited attention span at times, the examiner can allow a break, or when it appears that the child has a limited interest in completing the entire task, any number of the images may be used that tap into sport psychology themes or stimulus properties (see Chapter 3) the examiner wishes to assess.

Special considerations and limitations during administration

During and following the administration of images, one of the most important roles of the practitioner is to interpret responses. At first, interpretation is somewhat daunting, but like all assessments, repetition and the knowledge gleaned from each new assessment helps to build the necessary practitioner expertise to reap the benefits of using the AAT. Interpretation begins during the telling of stories. This interpretation can include identifying the level of projection and (practitioner) knowledge of other test scores, case notes, and interactions with the client. Adcock (1965) suggested that practitioners need to appreciate the difficulty of interpreting the degree of projection involved in a client's storytelling. Adcock also suggested that conclusions based solely on the responses of clients should be avoided, but rather conclusions and interpretations should be supplemented with the insight that has developed from dialogue-based interactions with the client. According to Eron (1959), "aside from the stimulus properties of the cards themselves, some other variables extraneous to the personality content of the individual subject contribute to a determination of both the formal and the content aspects of the productions" (p. 307). This interaction between the clinician and client is a critical component of the interpretation process and understanding of the level of projection.

> The problem with most projective tests is always the same; they allow the interpreter to project as much as the patient. Tests are essentially rulers for the purpose of measurement, but not all rulers are created with equal accuracy and durability. A tape ruler made of an elastic cord that can be stretched when readings are taken will yield different measurements depending on how far one stretches the cord. Not all people will pull the cord the same way. On the other hand, if a tape ruler were made of metal, no matter how one chose to pull the ruler, the measurements would not change due to one's strengths or weaknesses; therefore, external measurements of the world and other people will be less apt to be, influenced by the "pull" of the examiner.
>
> (Killian & Campbell, 1992, p. 425)

Interpretation of respondents' stories requires practitioners/therapists to be highly aware of their needs and projections. Similarly, *transference* and *counter-transference* also play important roles in the interpretation of participants' stories. Only a few researchers have addressed the issues of transference and counter-transference in the use of projective techniques mainly because these concepts are rarely discussed in personality assessment (Eron, 1959; Murstein, 1965). Transference is essentially a psychoanalytic term describing a process of actualisation of unconscious wishes. According to LaPlanche and Pontalis (1988), there are difficulties in defining transference because the term has become so broadly applied in clinical and counselling psychology. Transference is often used to explain *any* relationships clients have with their therapists. Freud first identified the psychological process of transference in the late 1800s. He observed that some clients presented strong feelings and fantasies about him that were not based in reality. Counter-transference is defined as "the whole of the analyst's unconscious reactions to the individual analysand [client]; especially to the analysand's own transference" (LaPlanche & Pontalis, 1988, p. 92). Some practitioners view counter-transference to include everything in the clinician's personality that could affect the treatment, whereas others believe counter-transference is restricted to unconscious processes bought about in the clinician by the transference of the client.

Eron (1959) addressed transference and counter-transference in relation to administration and interpretation of the TAT (and other projective). According to Eron, when clients feel they are in a permissive, accepting, non-critical, and non-evaluative situation, they are more likely to contribute fantasies in their storytelling. Practitioners can exercise some control over the clinical environment through the manner of instruction and their personal demeanours. Eron suggested that the presence of an examiner regardless of whether TAT stories are oral or written is an inhibiting factor in the production of strongly emotional material. Researchers have revealed that there are many variables (e.g., gender, age, social status, intelligence; Aronow et al., 2001) that affect TAT responses. This problem mainly occurs when there are substantial differences between the participant/client and the practitioner/therapist regarding those variables. As discussed briefly in Chapter 1, Eron also suggested there is a tendency to distort in storytelling due to the effects of transference. For example, participants may make conscious efforts to please practitioners and present themselves (impression management or self-deception) as specific kinds of people.

One final consideration for administration and interpretation relates to using the AAT cross-culturally where the psychologist and the athlete-client come from different cultural backgrounds. A thorough discussion of the issues of diversity and cultural contexts in using projective techniques is beyond the scope of this manual (see the "Diversity Issues" chapter in Aronow et al., 2001), but for a glimpse into some of the problems (and their resolutions), see Thompson and Andersen's (2012) story about a White New Zealander psychologist using the AAT with a Cook Islander football player.

Athlete Apperception Technique

Response booklet

IDENTIFYING INFORMATION

Name: ____

Sex: ______________________ Age: ___________________

Date: ______________ Administrator: ___________________

INSTRUCTIONS

This is a storytelling exercise that asks you to use your imagination and write a story about what is happening in the drawings (images) that you will see.

You will be shown a series of images one at a time.

Your job is to make up a story about each image.

In your story start by identifying who the central (main) character is.

Second, describe in detail what that person is thinking, and what that person is feeling right at this moment.

Then describe what is happening in the image, what events led up to this moment, and what the outcome will be (what do you think will happen?).

Write your story in the space provided for that image.

Please write as clearly as possible to make it easy for us to read (if you need more space, please write on the back of the paper as well).

Use your imagination and have fun making up the stories.

There are no right or wrong stories for these images; whatever you come up with will be just fine.

Do you have any questions before we begin?

Image 1 story

Write your story below. Write clearly, and please be sure your story includes:

- Who is the central (main) character?
- What are the central character's thoughts, feelings, and emotions?
- What is happening now?
- What led up to this moment?
- What will be the outcome?

Image 2 story

Write your story below. Write clearly, and please be sure your story includes:

- Who is the central (main) character?
- What are the central character's thoughts, feelings, and emotions?
- What is happening now?
- What led up to this moment?
- What will be the outcome?

Image 3 story

Write your story below. Write clearly, and please be sure your story includes:

- Who is the central (main) character?
- What are the central character's thoughts, feelings, and emotions?
- What is happening now?
- What led up to this moment?
- What will be the outcome?

Image 4 story

Write your story below. Write clearly, and please be sure your story includes:

- Who is the central (main) character?
- What are the central character's thoughts, feelings, and emotions?
- What is happening now?
- What led up to this moment?
- What will be the outcome?

Image 5 story

Write your story below. Write clearly, and please be sure your story includes:

- Who is the central (main) character?
- What are the central character's thoughts, feelings, and emotions?
- What is happening now?
- What led up to this moment?
- What will be the outcome?

Image 6 story

Write your story below. Write clearly, and please be sure your story includes:

- Who is the central (main) character?
- What are the central character's thoughts, feelings, and emotions?
- What is happening now?
- What led up to this moment?
- What will be the outcome?

Image 7 story

Write your story below. Write clearly, and please be sure your story includes:

- Who is the central (main) character?
- What are the central character's thoughts, feelings, and emotions?
- What is happening now?
- What led up to this moment?
- What will be the outcome?

Image 8 story

Write your story below. Write clearly, and please be sure your story includes:

- Who is the central (main) character?
- What are the central character's thoughts, feelings, and emotions?
- What is happening now?
- What led up to this moment?
- What will be the outcome?

Image 9 story

Write your story below. Write clearly, and please be sure your story includes:

- Who is the central (main) character?
- What are the central character's thoughts, feelings, and emotions?
- What is happening now?
- What led up to this moment?
- What will be the outcome?

Image 10 story

Write your story below. Write clearly, and please be sure your story includes:

- Who is the central (main) character?
- What are the central character's thoughts, feelings, and emotions?
- What is happening now?
- What led up to this moment?
- What will be the outcome?

Image 1S story

Write your story below. Write clearly, and please be sure your story includes:

- Who is the central (main) character?
- What are the central character's thoughts, feelings, and emotions?
- What is happening now?
- What led up to this moment?
- What will be the outcome?

Image 2S story

Write your story below. Write clearly, and please be sure your story includes:

- Who is the central (main) character?
- What are the central character's thoughts, feelings, and emotions?
- What is happening now?
- What led up to this moment?
- What will be the outcome?

Image 3S story

Write your story below. Write clearly, and please be sure your story includes:

- Who is the central (main) character?
- What are the central character's thoughts, feelings, and emotions?
- What is happening now?
- What led up to this moment?
- What will be the outcome?

Image 4S story

Write your story below. Write clearly, and please be sure your story includes:

- Who is the central (main) character?
- What are the central character's thoughts, feelings, and emotions?
- What is happening now?
- What led up to this moment?
- What will be the outcome?

Image 5S story

Write your story below. Write clearly, and please be sure your story includes:

- Who is the central (main) character?
- What are the central character's thoughts, feelings, and emotions?
- What is happening now?
- What led up to this moment?
- What will be the outcome?

Image 1C story

Write your story below. Write clearly, and please be sure your story includes:

- Who is the central (main) character?
- What are the central character's thoughts, feelings, and emotions?
- What is happening now?
- What led up to this moment?
- What will be the outcome?

Image 2C story

Write your story below. Write clearly, and please be sure your story includes:

- Who is the central (main) character?
- What are the central character's thoughts, feelings, and emotions?
- What is happening now?
- What led up to this moment?
- What will be the outcome?

Image 3C story

Write your story below. Write clearly, and please be sure your story includes:

- Who is the central (main) character?
- What are the central character's thoughts, feelings, and emotions?
- What is happening now?
- What led up to this moment?
- What will be the outcome?

Image 4C story

Write your story below. Write clearly, and please be sure your story includes:

- Who is the central (main) character?
- What are the central character's thoughts, feelings, and emotions?
- What is happening now?
- What led up to this moment?
- What will be the outcome?

Image 5C story

Write your story below. Write clearly, and please be sure your story includes:

- Who is the central (main) character?
- What are the central character's thoughts, feelings, and emotions?
- What is happening now?
- What led up to this moment?
- What will be the outcome?

Image 6C story

Write your story below. Write clearly, and please be sure your story includes:

- Who is the central (main) character?
- What are the central character's thoughts, feelings, and emotions?
- What is happening now?
- What led up to this moment?
- What will be the outcome?

References

Adcock, C. J. (1965). Thematic Apperception Test. In O. Buros (Ed.), *The sixth mental measurements yearbook* (pp. 533–535). Highland Park, NJ: Gryphon Press.
Aronow, E. (1995). Children's Apperceptive Story-Telling Test. In J. C. Conoley & J. C. Impara (Eds.), *The twelfth mental measurements yearbook* (pp. 180–181). Lincoln, NE: Buros Institute of Mental Measurements.
Aronow, E., Weiss, K. A., & Reznikoff, M. (2001). *A practical guide to the Thematic Apperception Test: The TAT in clinical practice*. Philadelphia, PA: Brunner-Routledge.
Bellak, L. (1950). The Thematic Apperception Test in clinical use. In L. E. Abt & L. Bellak (Eds.), *Projective psychology* (pp. 185–229). New York, NY: Grove Press.
Bellak, L., & Abrams, D. M. (1997). *The Thematic Apperception Test, the Children's Apperception Test, and the Senior Apperception Technique in clinical use* (6th ed.). Boston, MA: Allyn & Bacon.
Bellak, L., & Siegel, H. (1989). *The Children's Apperception Test (CAT)*. Needham Heights, MA: Allyn & Bacon.
Eron, L. D. (1959). Thematic Apperception Test. In O. Buros (Ed.), *The fifth mental measurements yearbook* (pp. 306–310). Highland Park, NJ: Gryphon Press.
Killian, G. A., & Campbell, B. M. (1992). Object Relations Technique. In D. J. Keyser & R. C. Sweetland (Eds.), *Test critiques* (Vol. IX, pp. 469–477). Austin, TX: PRO-ED.
LaPlanche, J., & Pontalis, J. B. (1988). *The language of psychoanalysis*. London, England: Hogarth Press.
Murray, H. A. (1943). *Thematic Apperception Test manual*. Cambridge, MA: Harvard University Press.
Murstein, B. I. (1965). The stimulus. In B. I. Murstein (Ed.), *Handbook of projective techniques* (pp. 509–546). New York, NY: Basic Books.
Rabin, A. I. (Ed.). (1968). *Projective techniques in personality assessment: A modern introduction*. New York, NY: Springer.
Ryan, R. M. (1985). Thematic Apperception Test. In D. J. Keyser & R. C. Sweetland (Eds.), *Test critiques* (Vol. II, pp. 799–814). Kansas City, MO: Westport.
Thompson, C., & Andersen, M. B. (2012). Moving toward Buddhist psychotherapy in sport: A case study. *The Sport Psychologist*, *26*, 624–643. doi:10.1123/tsp.26.4.624

5 Scoring and interpretation of projective techniques

AAT images can, at some times, with certain people in certain situations, evoke rich and elaborate stories and provide an in-depth and idiographic understanding of athletes' characteristics, motivations, and anxieties, and assist in the assessment of personality features. At other times, and with certain clients, there may be situations where the client has little interest or patience for a technique such as this one, and the exercise can be simply awkward and disheartening. We have, however, found that discussion of AAT responses is an excellent means for initiating dialogue, engaging the client, and possibly unmasking issues that might otherwise lie dormant. We expect there will be a wide range of experiences when administering the AAT image sets, and subsequently, a variety of experiences when scoring or interpreting the stories clients produce. Throughout his manual when we have talked about our suggestions for training to be able to interpret the AAT, and they are simply that: suggestions (please see "On interpretation" in Chapter 7).

The aim of this chapter is to present an example of how one might score the results of projective instruments such as the AAT. The development of the AAT was based on a belief that personality assessment should be inclusive of a variety of tools and methods to gain a clear understanding of an individual. The outcome of this work is the introduction of an idiographic projective technique for personality assessment with sports people. In Chapter 2, we presented two case examples that served to demonstrate administration, analysis, and interpretation of the AAT, but *scoring* (or more formally, measurement), that is, assigning numbers to various aspects of the data (stories) was not part of those processes. Given that one of the many reasons we produced the AAT was to offer it as an alternative to quantitative assessments, and to advocate assigning numbers to storytelling data seems antithetical to our purposes. One could argue that attempts to quantify TAT or AAT data, in part, stem from legitimisation pressures to appear "scientific" and apply classic quantitative, psychometric assessment principles (e.g., reliability, validity) to an instrument that did not evolve from positivistic roots such as IQ tests did. Projective techniques are fundamentally *qualitative* instruments, and when they are subjected, in a procrustean manner, to fit quantitative standards of objectively scored assessment tests, a fundamental mismatch occurs. In essence, a quantification of qualitative data strikes us as somewhat odd and not especially helpful unless one is trying to do some nomothetic research with an idiographic instrument. Nevertheless, quantification of the TAT and other projective technique data has a long history, and we felt obliged to include at least one example of a numbers-based scoring system for readers interested in quantification or for those wanting to know more details and processes of other scoring systems.

Interpretation (and scoring) of the Thematic Apperception Test

Shneidman (1999) suggested there are various approaches to thematic test analysis that can be devised to emphasise the elements (or aspects) of the stories, and the elements (or aspects) of the characters. The major methods that clinicians may use during administration and interpretation of the TAT can be subsumed into five categories: normative, hero-oriented, intuitive, interpersonal, and perceptual. The first, *normative* technique is used primarily to quantify thematic test interpretation. The basic operation is to compare tabulations derived from the test protocol of the person being studied with normative data. The general purpose of normative testing with projective techniques is more often personality research than psychodiagnostic service. The *hero-oriented* method is where interpreters concentrate on the chief protagonist in the stories. This approach emphasises the story hero or heroine (e.g., their defining needs, pressures, defences). This approach also focuses on feelings, interactions, relations to other story characters and ego activities. The *intuitive* approach is the most unstructured of the methods to analyse thematic instruments. With the intuitive approach there is a reliance on the insightful empathy of the interpreter, and also a free association of the clinician's unconscious against the blackboard of the technique's protocol (Shneidman, 1999).

A further method some clinicians use during administration and interpretation is the *interpersonal* approach. This approach comprises three variations in method. Using the first variation, the interpersonal situations of the characters in the stories are analysed. For the second method, the attention is focused on directed interpersonal feelings (e.g., hostility, warmth, flight) among the story characters and from the respondent toward the characters. With the third variation, the respondents' social perceptions of their stories' characters and interactions are the central aspects of the analysis. The *perceptual* approach relates to the formal aspects of the respondent's production such as distortions of visual stimuli of technique materials, idiosyncratic use of language, peculiarities of thought or logic, or loose or bizarre twists within the story itself (Shneidman, 1999). Each of these approaches places a different emphasis on aspects of the narratives and various elements of the characters introduced.

Clinicians and researchers who use the TAT differ in how they employ the tool as source material for uncovering characteristics of the clients/participants they believe are significant. For example, a clinician may use the TAT solely to determine diagnostic characterisations of behaviour or to locate important emotional relationships in a person's world. According to Rotter (1946), interpretations from the TAT should be considered only as working hypotheses or leads for further investigation, and "the value, significance, nature, and validity of the tests are dependent upon the interpreter, his experience, and his approach to the field of personality" (p. 206). Many clinicians who regularly use the TAT do not consider it a self-sufficient assessment tool (Rapaport, Gill, & Schafer, 1986). Thus, in clinical assessment, the TAT is often used as part of a larger battery of tests and interview data. Clinicians can assess background and convergent information in light of the TAT responses. In clinical use, stories are interpreted in accordance with general principles of inference derived from psychodynamic theory.

There have been numerous attempts to develop scoring systems for the TAT, but Rapaport et al. (1986) suggested there are no specific rules that apply to the scoring of the TAT. "These techniques are not hard and fast rules like those of scoring other tests, they are rather like viewpoints for looking upon the TAT stories that must become ingrained in the examiner, so that he can use them flexibly and judiciously" (p. 490). Ryan (1985) believed that the TAT was not necessarily a test but rather a method, "one with considerable adaptability and generative capacities" (p. 812). Murray originally used his *personology* theory to apply a scoring system, and several other scoring schemes are currently available. Some of the better-known scoring systems have come from the work of Arnold (1962), Bellak and Abrams (1997), Dana (1982), Eron (1950), McClelland, Atkinson, Clarke, and Lowell (1953), Rapaport et al. (1986), Veroff (1958), and Wyatt (1947). For a review of a large number of TAT scoring systems, see Jenkins (2008). According to Ryan, many researchers and clinicians developed unique scoring schemes based on their theoretical frameworks. Some of these scoring systems are quantitative whereas others are qualitative, or a combination of both. Some of these systems are oriented primarily toward scoring story content, whereas others focus on more formal aspects such as the construction of the stories, the qualities of the characters, and the relationships between the characters. The good news for practitioners new to projective techniques is that there are a life-time of readings and resources available as well as the knowledge that, much like the instructions we give to clients during AAT administration, there is not a "right or wrong" way to do it. We are also keen to hear from practitioners working with the AAT and provide further guidance if necessary.

Potential scoring system for the AAT

We have already presented some examples of analysis and interpretation of AAT images using: a content import method, a comparison of responses with the stimulus properties of the image, sport psychology thematic analysis, and psychodynamic interpretations in Chapter 2 (see also Chapter 3 for the stimulus properties of the images). Here we will focus briefly on one quantitative scoring system that could be applied to the AAT.

One example of a contemporary scoring scheme for TAT stories is the Social Cognition and Object Relations Scale (SCORS; Westen, 1995; Westen, Lohr, Silk, Kerber, & Goodrich, 1989). The SCORS, although developed primarily for scoring the TAT, can be adapted for use with most projective storytelling techniques according to Westen et al. The current SCORS consists of eight dimensions: (a) complexity of representations of people, (b) affective quality of representations, (c) capacity for emotional investment in relationships, (d) emotional investment in values and moral standards, (e) understanding social causality, (f) experience and management of aggressive impulses, (g) self-esteem, and (h) identity and coherence of the self. See Figure 5.1 for an example of two SCORS dimensions that could be used to quantify and interpret the AAT, the AAT-S, and the AAT-C. Each dimension is rated on a Likert scale of 1 (low-level functioning) to 7 (high-level functioning). A raw score (1 to 7) is given for each dimension, for each image. Scores are then totalled for each dimension, and a mean score for each dimension is derived. For example, on the *self-esteem* dimension, scores for each AAT and AAT-S image (15 images) would be summed (e.g., 5 + 5 + 7 + 5 + 5 + 5 + 7 + 5 + 5 + 5 + 7 + 5 + 5 + 5 + 5 = 81). The total is then divided by the number of images scored (e.g., 81/15 = 5.4). Higher scores indicate mature and healthy functioning. According to Westen, the SCORS represents an *object-relations* approach. The SCORS is used to rate responses on a number of dimensions that may co-vary. A person could be high on some dimensions, such as management of aggressive feelings but low on others such as investment in relationships.

The SCORS has been applied to a variety of projective techniques. Validity has been established by comparison of SCORS results with clinician assessments and self-report measures such as the Minnesota Multiphasic Personality Inventory (MMPI; Hathaway & Mckinley, 1940). According to

Complexity of representations of people:

1 = tends to be grossly egocentric or to confuse his/her own thoughts, feelings, or attributes with others';

3 = views the self and others with little subtlety or complexity; descriptions of people tend to be sparse, simple, one-dimensional, poorly integrated, or split into all-good or all-bad;

5 = views of the self and others have some depth and complexity but are relatively conventional; is able to see people's strengths as well as weaknesses and to take others' perspectives;

7 = is psychologically minded; views of people are subtle, rich, and complex.

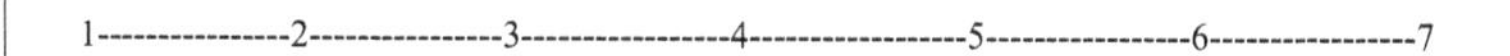

Capacity for emotional investment in relationships:

1 = tends to focus primarily on his/her own needs in relationships; to have unstable, tumultuous relationships; or to have few if any relationships;

3 = relationships tend to be shallow, lacking in depth, or based primarily on mutual participation in shared activity or mutual self-interest;

5 = demonstrates conventional sentiments of friendship, caring, love, and empathy in relationships;

7 = tends to have deep, committed relationships characterized by mutual sharing, emotional intimacy, interdependence, respect, and appreciation.

Figure 5.1 Example of the dimensions of the SCORS for interviews and other narrative data

Karp, Holmstrom, and Silber (1989), inter-rater reliabilities for the SCORS have been obtained in the .80 to .98 range. The authors of the Apperceptive Personality Test (APT; Holmstrom, Silber, & Karp, 1990) have studied and used the SCORS in conjunction with the APT images. Holmstrom et al. compared two studies with college students using TAT cards 7GF, 3GF, 7BM, 8BM, 6BM, 4, 9BM, and 14. Those seven TAT cards were used because of comparability with APT cards regarding the age and gender characteristics portrayed. Holmstrom et al. used the standard APT format for both instruments, with the SCORS being applied to the stories gathered. The primary finding was that the APT and TAT elicited a similar range of psychological themes. The SCORS should be an applicable scoring option for use with the AAT. One warning Westen (1995) issued was that the coding of stories using the SCORS should be undertaken by experienced and psychologically minded practitioners, with preferably two raters. According to Aronow, Weiss, and Reznikoff (2001), the system developed by Westen, although time-consuming, shows both good criterion-related and construct validity.

We imagine that most applied sport and exercise psychologists who choose to use the AAT will probably not quantify the stories produced, but we wanted to present, however briefly, at least one way that a researcher or practitioner could go about assigning numbers to AAT data. We have referenced a wide variety to scoring systems for readers to check out, especially Jenkins (2008), and we chose to present the SCORS (Westen, 2002) because it stems from a psychodynamic framework (i.e., object relations), which is most congruent with our approach in constructing the AAT.

References

Arnold, M. B. (1962). *Story sequence analysis: A new method of measuring motivation and predicting achievement*. New York, NY: Columbia University Press.

Aronow, E., Weiss, K. A., & Reznikoff, M. (2001). *A practical guide to the Thematic Apperception Test: The TAT in clinical practice*. Philadelphia, PA: Brunner-Routledge.

Bellak, L., & Abrams, D. M. (1997). *The Thematic Apperception Test, the Children's Apperception Test, and the Senior Apperception Technique in clinical use* (6th ed.). Boston, MA: Allyn & Bacon.

Dana, R. H. (1982). *A human science model for personality assessment with projective techniques*. Springfield, IL: Charles C. Thomas.

Eron, L. D. (1950). A normative study of the Thematic Apperception Test. *Psychological Monographs*, *64*(9), i–48. doi:10.1037/h0093627

Hathaway, S. R., & McKinley, J. C. (1940). A multiphasic personality schedule (Minnesota): 1. Construction of the schedule. *Journal of Psychology*, *10*, 249–254. doi: 10.1080/00223980.1940.9917000

Holmstrom, R. W., Silber, D. E., & Karp, S. A. (1990). Development of the Apperceptive Personality Test. *Journal of Personality Assessment*, *54*, 252–264. Available from http://www.tandfonline.com/doi/abs/10.1080/00223891.1990.9673991

Jenkins, S. R. (Ed.). (2008). *A handbook of clinical scoring systems for Thematic Apperceptive Techniques*. New York, NY: Routledge.

Karp, S. A., Holmstrom, R. W., & Silber, D. E. (1989). *The Apperceptive Personality Test manual*. Worthington, OH: International Diagnostic Systems.

McClelland, D. C., Atkinson, J. W., Clarke, R. A., & Lowell, E. L. (1953). *The achievement motive*. Englewood Cliffs, NJ: Prentice-Hall.

Rapaport, D., Gill, M. M., & Schafer, R. (1986). *Diagnostic psychological testing*. New York, NY: International Universities Press.

Rotter, J. B. (1946). Thematic Apperception Tests: Suggestions for administration and interpretation. *Journal of Personality*, *15*, 70–92. doi:10.1111/j.1467–6494.1946.tb01052.x

Ryan, R. M. (1985). Thematic Apperception Test. In D. J. Keyser & R. C. Sweetland (Eds.), *Test critiques* (Vol. II, pp. 799–814). Kansas City, MO: Westport.

Shneidman, E. S. (1999). The Thematic Apperception Test: A paradise of psychodynamics. In L. Geiser & M. I. Stein (Eds.), *Evocative images: The Thematic Apperception Test and the art of projection* (pp. 87–97). Washington, DC: American Psychological Association.

Veroff, J. (1958). A scoring manual for the power motive. In J. W. Atkinson (Ed.), *Motives in fantasy, action, and society* (pp. 219–233). Princeton, NJ: VanNostrand.

Westen, D. (1995). *Revision of Social Cognition and Object Relations Scale: Q-sort for projective stories (SCORS—Q)*. Unpublished manuscript, Department of Psychiatry, The Cambridge Hospital and Harvard Medical School, Cambridge, MA.

Westen, D. (2002). *SCORS manual for narratives*. Atlanta, GA: Emory University Press.

Westen, D., Lohr, N., Silk, K., Kerber, K., & Goodrich, S. (1989). *Object relations and social cognition TAT scoring manual* (4th ed.). Unpublished manuscript, University of Michigan, Ann Arbor.

Wyatt, F. (1947). The scoring and analysis of the Thematic Apperception Test. *Journal of Psychology*, *24*, 319–330. doi:10.1080/00223980.1947.9917359

6 The AAT image sets

During the early stages in the development of the AAT, our major aim was to cultivate particular images that tap athlete- and sport-specific dispositions, complexes, and themes. Following the progressive reduction of a large number of sport images (discussed in detail in Chapter 2), this work has culminated in the three general image sets below: (a) an adult image set (AAT: 10 images); (b) a supplementary set (AAT-S: 5 images); and a children's set (AAT-C: 6 images). The images are presented below in a full-page landscape format. They can be cut directly from this book or photocopied (or downloaded from the e-version), and then pasted on cards or laminated; essentially, they are yours to do with as you choose. One further recommendation is to remove the *image number* from the image itself as this may become a distraction to the respondent, or be unwittingly incorporated into the story. See the basic projective test administration suggestions we have outlined in Chapter 4.

Image 1

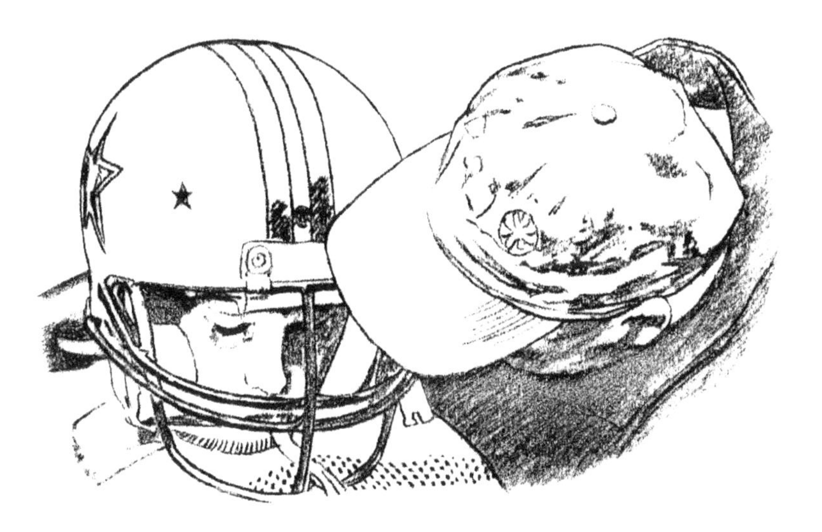

Image 2 and Image 2C

Image 3

Image 4

Image 5

Image 6 and Image 6C

Image 7

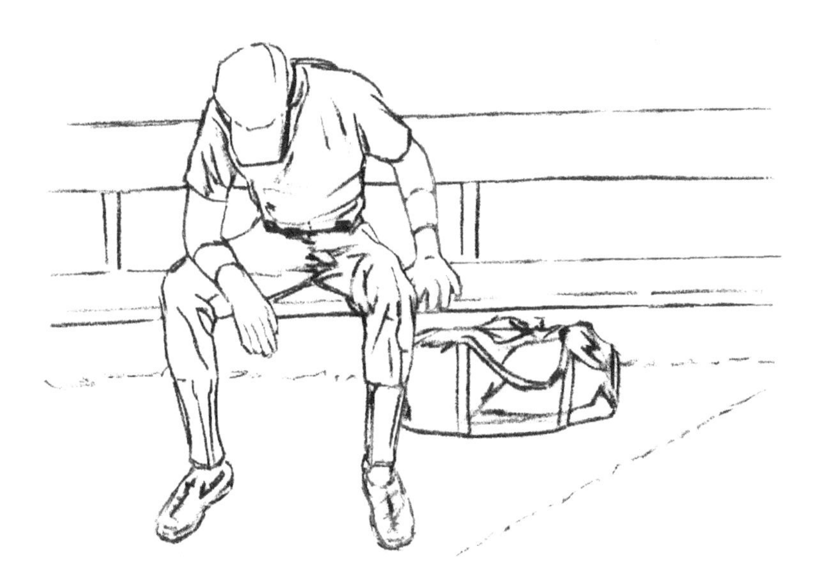

Image 8

Image 9

Image 10

AAT-S: supplementary set

Image 1S

Image 2S

Image 3S

Image 4S

Image 5S and Image 3C

AAT-C: children's set

This set contains six images in total; three new images, two images from the original set (AAT Image 2 and AAT Image 6), and one image from the supplementary set (AAT-S Image 5S). Included below are the three new images (Image 1C, Image 4C, and Image 5C); Image 2C, Image 3C, and Image 6C are above.

Image 1C

Image 4C

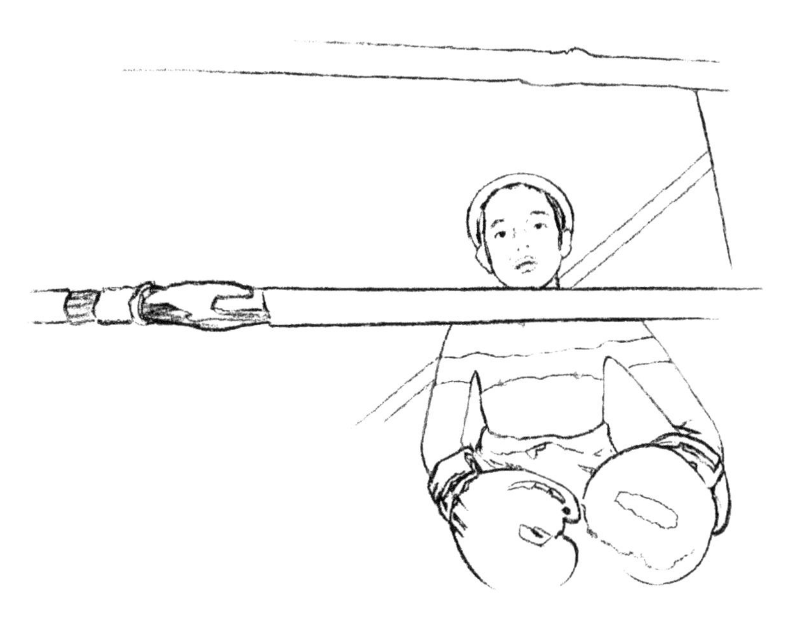

Image 5C

7 Final thoughts on using the AAT

In this last chapter, and in keeping with the spirit of the AAT, we would like to tell some stories about storytelling. The tales and accounts that clients construct in psychotherapy, sport psychology practice, and other forms of interpersonal and talking treatments are often prompted by specific questions or requests for information from practitioners (e.g., "Please tell me more about the last time you became anxious during competition."), or they are client initiated (e.g., "I have to talk to you about what happened at the tournament."). These stories are sometimes cognitive, linear reconstructions of events relatively devoid of emotional content. At other times, the tales are filled with turmoil, shame, and dread. The spectrum of storytelling is vast and covers sombre indigo, burning orange, calming aquamarine, and even invisible (unconscious) infrared. The client telling her tale is in a kind of theatrical performance, and she embellishes (or diminishes) the narrative through all sorts of verbal and non-verbal behaviours such as rate of speech, voice inflections, facial expressions, body movements, pauses, eye contact (or avoidance) with the therapist, emotional displays, visual evidence of activation (e.g., blushing), changing breathing patterns, and so forth, many of which are manifested unconsciously. Often contained within those stories are unvoiced questions for the audience (e.g., the sport psychologist, the psychotherapist) such as: "Now that I have told you this horrible tale, will you think me awful and abandon me?"

As practitioners, we can glean useful information from our clients' verbal stories and their "epi-narrative" (if we are allowed to coin a term) ornamentations of non-verbal behaviours and unvoiced questions. We can also make observations and tentative interpretations of the unconscious content bubbling underneath and occasionally breaking through, often somatically. Moreover, for the psychodynamically bent practitioner, questions arise as to whether the tale and its epi-narrative accoutrements have something significant to say about the relationship between the client and the practitioner (known as "derivative" stories that unconsciously symbolise the interpersonal configuration or therapeutic situation). The narratives told in therapy are generally reality based, even dreams, in that the dreams happened to the clients.

Something different, however, occurs when we ask clients to engage in fantasy storytelling as in the *miracle questions* from motivational interviewing (e.g., If a miracle happened, and overnight everything you wanted to change came about, then what would that be like?) or when we ask for story construction in response to an image from the AAT. We are requesting that our clients engage their creative faculties and begin a process that probably evolved for our species relatively shortly after the birth of language.

When we tell stories about ourselves to our therapists or sport psychologists, our protective, censoring, and defensive faculties may be more or less active. At the beginning of a relationship with a sport psychologist, those faculties may be dominant and substantially colour the stories told in wishful thinking, self-delusion, and impression management. As trust, respect, caring, unconditional positive regard, safety, and yes, even love, develop, those protective features' sway over our narratives will likely diminish, and the stories will get closer to our hearts, our deepest desires, and our most abject fears. Nevertheless, when we are asked to "spin yarns" about hypothetical others in a picture, those protective faculties can be easily bypassed because the story "is not about me." This bypassing of internal censors helps suppressed (or repressed) trauma, hearts' (unacceptable) desires, rage at perceived injustices, and paralysing self-doubts (among many other intrapersonal phenomena) come flowing out in a type of personal fairy tale. Just as *Little Red Riding Hood* is both a story of misadventures in the woods and a horrifying tale of the consequences of giving in to sexual and aggressive impulses, so too is an AAT story something more than a hero's narrative of hard work, adversity, and failure in the end. It may be a tale that serves as a stand-in for decades of being told one is never good enough, one is not worthy of love, and one is not desirable, no matter how hard one works. It could be a story of taking on the impossible task of making a depressed parent happy, only to fail again and again. Which one is it? It could be both. Stories stimulated by AAT images are often multi-multi-layered. We don't know what any individual story is about, but with the responses to 6 or 8 or 10 images, clinical judgement, and strong therapeutic relationship building, where the story fits in the mosaic of a client's life may begin to emerge.

Asking clients to engage in fantasy storytelling probably involves more parts of the brain than a linear construction of past personal events. Storytelling and story hearing capture us, and they are part of our evolutionary history. As Cozolino (2010) suggested:

> The evolution of the human brain is inextricably interwoven with the expansion of culture and the emergence of language. Thus, it is

> no coincidence that human beings are storytellers. Through countless generations, humans have gathered to listen to stories of the hunt, the exploits of their ancestors, and morality tales of good and evil. It has long been supposed that these stories support the transmission of culture while promoting psychological and emotional stability. Stories connect us to others, prop up our often fragile identities, and keep our brains regulated. Thus, . . . both the urge to tell a tale and our vulnerability to being captivated by one are deeply woven into the structures of our brains. . . . [Narratives] serve as powerful tools for high-level neural network integration. The combination of linear storyline and visual imagery woven together with verbal and nonverbal expressions of emotion activates and utilizes dedicated circuitry of both left and right hemispheres, cortical and subcortical networks, the various regions of the frontal lobes, and the hippocampus and amygdala. The cooperative and interactive activation involved in stories may be precisely what is required for sculpting and maintaining neural network integration while allowing us to combine sensations, feelings, and behaviors with conscious awareness. Further, stories link individuals into families, tribes, and nations and into a group mind linking each individual brain. It is likely that our brains have been able to become as complex as they are precisely because of the power of narratives and the group to support neural integration.
>
> (pp. 163–164)

When we ask for stories in response to AAT cards, we are tapping into something that, in a way, almost defines our species. Story production and storytelling activate and integrate many areas and functions of the brain, and, when told in the presence of a compassionate, present, caring, non-judgmental other, can down-regulate distressing limbic activations and can be a therapeutic experience.

The AAT as a therapeutic encounter

Projective methods have been used for over a century in psychiatry, and clinical psychology and going back well before Hermann Rorschach (1921) burst onto the scene with his inkblots and his book *Psychodiagnostik*. The original goals of using these methods were to explore psychopathology, assess personality, and contribute to diagnoses. The information gleaned from projective techniques was also used to help with developing treatment plans. Rosenzweig (1948), however, suggested that the TAT could be usefully incorporated into the therapeutic process by asking clients to make their own interpretations of what the stories they told might mean and how they might be saying something about their current difficulties. More recently, Drum (1992) suggested that a shift has happened in how:

> counselors and psychologists are conceptualizing and implementing assessment procedures. . . . [moving toward] a belief that assessment activities should not stand outside the change process; rather, they should blend into treatment strategies to guide self-discovery and to inform clients. This represents a clear shift from *assessment-for-treatment* to *assessment-in-treatment.*
>
> (p. 622)

In regards to projective techniques as integrated into therapeutic processes and potentially helpful in the development of working alliances in therapy, Goldman (1992) suggested that projective methods provide a means of:

> helping clients to know and understand themselves better – methods that are flexible, open-ended, holistic, and non-statistical . . . and thereby tap values, interests, and needs in ways that standardized tests do not. Because these activities involve the client actively, they can flow directly out of and back into the counseling relationship.
>
> (p. 616)

Moreover, Schor (2003) also supplied a strong rationale for the use of projective techniques within a therapy framework:

> By discussing these observations [projective story interpretations] with the therapist, the client may develop an increased ability to reflect and observe the patterns of thoughts, feelings, and actions as they occur. The client may be more likely to continue to engage in this form of perspective-taking outside the therapy setting.
>
> (p. 46)

The client can take what was learned through projective techniques into the real world and apply that knowledge. As we tell our clients repeatedly: what happens during the therapy hour, or the sport psychology session, is only a small part of the process – a time to discuss, explore, tweak, and then develop plans and social, cognitive, and behavioural experiments to take into the world and try out. The "real" therapy is *out there* 7 days a week, not *in here* during 1-hour appointments.

In the applied sport psychology literature, there is one example of using projective techniques within a psychotherapy framework to the benefit of the client, a sport psychology doctoral student, and their therapeutic relationship (we discussed this briefly in Chapter 4) Thompson and Andersen (2012) described the work of a Pakeha (White) New Zealander sport psychology intern and his Pacific Islander rugby client. The student conducted the AAT with his client, and being new to projective methods, he struggled with interpretations and seeing meaningful themes behind what seemed, at first, to be fairly short and straight-forward simple narratives. In supervision with his psychodynamically oriented supervisor, however, his blind spots as a member of the dominant White ethnic group became apparent, and those "simple tales" began to take on substantial cultural meaning reflecting the conflicts, frustrations, and hyper vigilance of a member of an oppressed minority. By using the AAT as a clinical tool, the doctoral student was able to see and confront his prejudices and stereotypes and how they diminished and impoverished his interpretations of his client's tales. He used his experience in supervision to express his ignorance (and desire to learn more) of the life experiences of Pacific Islanders to his client, and his admitting to *not knowing* and inviting his client to be his teacher helped deepen their therapeutic bond. The student grew as a practitioner as did his relationship with the rugby player. Discussing the AAT images and stories together led to the client becoming even more engaged in therapy than he had been before the AAT. Thompson and Andersen wrote:

> I [Thompson] suggested [to the client, Dave] that disappointment and a sense of failure come through strongly in the stories, but perhaps his self-blame at his reported poor performance may have affected what he saw in the cards. A truthful transcript of this session would show my hesitation when mentioning these emotions, probably indicating my lingering discomfort in discussing his depression. Dave's reply surprised me. He said, "Look, whatever you see in these stories, please give it to me straight, I can take it, you don't need to hold anything back." His words made me aware of his vulnerability at submitting to a projective test of this kind. Dave had learned to be guarded and ashamed of his emotions, but he now seemed willing to confront them.
>
> (p. 633)

Here, the client is ready to jump into the therapeutic process, and he helps the doctoral student overcome his trepidations about exploring depressive content. The AAT was a vehicle for both client and intern to become more engaged in therapeutic processes than they had been before, and it helped both of them grow. The sort of collaboration seen in the Thompson and Andersen (2012) article shows how the AAT has the potential to influence one of the common overarching goals of therapy, and that is the *re-storying* of the client's experiences (or whole life) in ways that the new story, or self-narrative, is more self-compassionate, accepting, and happier than early versions of character deficits, unworthiness of love, and horrible personal equations such as *good performance = good person.*

On interpretation

Throughout this manual, we have emphasised the psychoanalytic foundations for the development of the AAT along with psychodynamic interpretations of the stories clients generate. We have also suggested that gaining a substantial background in psychoanalytic theory would help practitioners interested in using the AAT, but, our suggestions for training for using the AAT are, as we wrote earlier, just that: *suggestions*. We are not fond of orthodoxy in most all of its forms, and we see no compelling reason why someone would need a psychodynamic background to use the AAT as an adjunct to treatment, as a topic and demonstration in a graduate sport psychology seminar, or as an instrument used in qualitative research. When we make psychoanalytic interpretations of a group of stories our clients tell, we are also involved in another kind of projection: we take psychodynamic theory and then *impose* (project) it upon the narratives. This process is much like a qualitative researcher who interviews participants with a theory in mind and then interprets those conversations through that chosen lens. Gucciardi and Gordon (2009) did something similar with personal construct theory (Kelly, 1955/1991) applied to athletes and exercisers, and the result was a thoughtful and useful contribution to our literature.

Sport psychologists with different theoretical predilections such as the big-five personality theory (Wiggins, 1996), self-determination theory (SDT; Sheldon, Williams, & Joiner, 2003), or Gestalt therapy (Perls, 1972) could easily apply their models or theories to the interpretations of AAT narratives. For example, an SDT interpretation of AAT stories, exploring the contents for themes related to intrinsic and extrinsic motivations and the needs for autonomy, relatedness, and competence, could be helpful in understanding athletes' worlds and in assisting clients in (re)constructing their self-narratives through an SDT lens. As we tell our students, "All theories and models are wrong, but many are useful. Find one that resonates with you, and become an expert." We cannot think of a situation where a sport psychologist's specific bent or preference could not be applied to the interpretation of client-generated AAT material. When it comes to theories or models applied to AAT narratives, we consider the technique to be an equal-opportunity instrument amenable for use with whatever theory resonates with the practitioner choosing to administer it to athlete/coach clients.

The AAT and the qualitative sport psychology researcher

We suggested, in Chapter 2, that the AAT could be useful in certain types of qualitative research in sport and exercise psychology, particularly case-study research, life history approaches, and narrative analysis studies. In general, any qualitative research that involves storytelling might be augmented with (or enhanced by) using the AAT as a supplementary source of both data and interactions between participants and researchers. There is a doctoral thesis in the public domain that has done just that (Kavanagh, 2010; go to http://vuir.vu.edu.au/15549/). The researcher first conducted an in-depth interview with a former tennis player who transitioned into coaching roles, and then she did a thematic content analysis of the data. Later she re-visited the participant, Craig, and worked with him on 10 of the AAT images. Here is how Kavanagh described her reflections on using the AAT in research:

> Craig's AAT responses complemented, clarified, and added to his in-depth interview. They revealed valuable clues about his characteristics, motivations, and anxieties that would have been difficult to access with an interview or another assessment tool. Furthermore, the AAT images were helpful for engaging Craig. The intent of the test was not particularly obvious, and it gave him considerable freedom to generate responses. He seemed generally more relaxed than during his in-depth interview. . . . There were some cautions or limitations that I noted during the research process. First, I would not have been able to interpret Craig's AAT responses without the insight from his in-depth interview. Consequently, it is my opinion that the AAT should not be used as a stand-alone instrument, but rather, in conjunction with other sources of information. Furthermore, the AAT images evoke material of a highly emotional and personal nature. For this reason, psychologists need to be aware of their own knowledge limitations and take reasonable care when interpreting the information from projective instruments. I believe the AAT has the potential to be over-interpreted and could be used irresponsibly. Finally, psychologists need to be mindful of the role they play in the process, and take steps to understand how their own "stuff" contributes to the administration and interpretation of the AAT. One of the major lessons I learned was that projective tests allow the interpreter to project as much as the participant.
>
> (p. 144)

Although Kavanagh did not use the AAT in the intensely collaborative way that Thompson and Andersen (2012) did (she was not conducting a psychotherapy case study), she did find using the instrument helped engage her participant, and it also brought some added depth to the Craig's tale. We think all of Kavanagh's warnings in the above quote about the AAT should be kept in mind for anyone using the technique in research or applied work.

In narrative analysis research (see Smith & Sparkes, 2009), which has recently gained popularity in sport and exercise psychology inquiry, there would appear to be plenty of room to augment the research paradigm with storytelling generation techniques such as the AAT. In simplified terms, narrative analysis involves at least two people: the storyteller (research participant usually telling tales about certain aspects of her experiences), and the narrative analyst who engages in the academic task of interpreting/analysing the research participant's stories. The storytelling and the analysis usually take place in two different actual and metaphorical locations: storytelling in a comfortable research interview room and analysis at a computer in the researcher's office (or at home with a glass of wine). This distance is not a flaw or a criticism of the research paradigm, but how the AAT might contribute to this research method is to close that distance by doing the qualitative research equivalent of what Rosenzweig (1948) suggested for the use of the TAT in therapy: engage and help the research participant partake in her own analysis of the AAT stories, what they might mean, and what they might say about her current situation. In this way, the narrative analysis of the participant's stories truly becomes co-constructed, and the participant is invited to story and re-story his experiences in what we hope is a non-judgmental, loving, and caring encounter with the researcher (see Andersen & Ivarsson, 2016).We believe, there are numerous niches for the AAT in an inclusive sport and exercise psychology research landscape.

Drawing the curtain on our tale

Jaques in Shakespeare's *As You Like It* said, "All the world's a stage," and the metaphor of drawing a curtain suggests there was a production or a performance of storytelling that has come to an end. There have been many stages, both temporal and metaphorical, in the development of the AAT. There was the academic stage of completing a PhD with all its, as Polonius in *Hamlet* would say, "tragical–comical–historical–pastoral" features. And, maybe to the main point here, there is the performance stage of presenting the AAT to the sport, exercise, and clinical psychology communities. We are understandably concerned about what the critics of our production might have to say. Was our story compelling and convincing? Were the production values (e.g., the images) high enough? Was there something that touched the near universal in the human story? We don't know the answers to these questions, but we draw our own curtain on this "stage" of the play for now. We do hope, however, that other practitioners and researchers will produce sequels to this tale through their writing, and who knows? We may write some too.

References

Andersen, M. B., & Ivarsson, A. (2016). A methodology of loving kindness: How interpersonal neurobiology, compassion, and transference can inform researcher-participant encounters and storytelling. *Qualitative Research in Sport, Exercise and Health*, *8*, 1–20. doi:10.1080/2159676X.2015.1056827

Cozolino, L. (2010). *The neuroscience of psychotherapy: Healing the social brain* (2nd ed.). New York, NY: Norton.

Drum, D. J. (1992). A review of Leo Goldman's article "Qualitative assessment: An approach for counselors." *Journal of Counseling & Development*, *70*, 622–623. doi:10.1002/j.1556-6676.1992.tb01672.x

Goldman, L. (1992). Qualitative assessment: An approach for counselors. *Journal of Counseling & Development*, *70*, 616–621. doi:10.1002/j.1556–6676.1992.tb01671.x

Gucciardi, D. F., & Gordon, S. (2009). Construing the athlete and exerciser: Research and applied perspectives from personal construct theory. *Journal of Applied Sport Psychology*, *21*(Suppl. 1), S17–S33. doi:10.1080/10413200802582821

Kavanagh, T. E. (2010). *Transitions to the other side of the net: Tales of tennis players who become coaches* (Unpublished doctoral dissertation). Victoria University, Melbourne, VIC, Australia. Available from http://vuir.vu.edu.au/15549/

Kelly, G. A. (1991). *The psychology of personal constructs: A theory of personality* (Vol. I). London, England: Routledge. (Original work published 1955.)

Perls, F. S. (1972). *Gestalt therapy verbatim*. New York, NY: Bantam Books.

Rorschach, H. (1921). *Psychodiagnostik*. Bern, Switzerland: Bircher.

Rosenzweig, S. (1948). The Thematic Apperception Technique in diagnosis and therapy. *Journal of Personality*, *16*, 437–444. doi:10.1111/j.1467–6494.1948.tb02299.x

Schor, L. (2003). A person-centered approach to the use of projectives in counseling. *The Person-Centered Journal*, *10*, 39–48.

Sheldon, K. M., Williams, G., & Joiner, T. (2003). *Self-determination theory in the clinic: Motivating physical and mental health*. New Haven, CT: Yale University Press.

Smith, B., & Sparkes, A. C. (2009). Narrative analysis and sport and exercise psychology: Understanding lives in diverse ways. *Psychology of Sport and Exercise*, *10*, 279–288. doi:10.1016/j.psychsport.2008.07.012

Thompson, C., & Andersen, M. B. (2012). Moving towards Buddhist psychotherapy in sport: A case study. *The Sport Psychologist*, *26*, 624–643. doi:10.1123/tsp.26.4.624

Wiggins, J. S. (Ed.). (1996). *The five-factor model of personality: Theoretical perspectives*. New York, NY: Guilford Press.

Index

www.ingramcontent.com/pod-product-compliance
Ingram Content Group UK Ltd.
Pitfield, Milton Keynes, MK11 3LW, UK
UKHW020416010325
455677UK00029B/913